STUDIES IN INDIAN WRITING IN ENGLISH

STUDIES IN INDIAN WRITING IN ENGLISH

With a Focus on Indian English Drama

P. Bayapa Reddy

PRESTIGE

Published by
Prestige Books
3/28, East Patel Nagar, New Delhi 110 008
in association with
Indian Society for Commonwealth Studies
New Delhi

ISBN: 81-85218-26-9

Jacket design by
3-A Corporation,
New Delhi 110 002

Phototypesetting by
data culture
New Delhi 110 065
Ph. 6431070

Printed at
Mehra Offset Press
New Delhi 110 002

Contents

Drama with a Message: A.S.P. Ayyar's *Sita's Choice*

A.S. Panchapakesa Ayyar was born on 26 January 1899 at Ayilam village in Kerala. He was the author of five plays, four novels, a few volumes of shorter fiction, books of essays and philosophy.

Having received education in various institutions at Kottayi, Palghat, Trivandrum and Madras, Ayyar went to England on a Tata scholarship in 1919 and obtained a degree in Law. During his stay in England for three years, he passed the I.C.S examination. Later, he made two trips to England and was elected a Fellow of The Royal Society of Literature of the United Kingdom in 1933. Though he started his career as District Collector and District Magistrate, he opted for Judiciary where he became Justice of the Madras High Court (1948-49). As a judge, he was known for his spirit of independence and ardent nationalist views.

The greatest of Ayyar's novels are *Chanakya and Chandragupta* (1951) and *Baladitya* (1954). His portrayal of Chanakya is a magnificent piece of characterization. His *Rambles in Art,* his edition of *Two Plays of Bhasa* and his monograph on Bhasa reveal his critical acumen. His five published plays are *In the Clutch of the Devil, Sita's Choice, The Slave of Ideas, A Mother's Sacrifice* and *The Trial of Science for the Murder of Humanity*. He died on April 11, 1963 in Madras.

A.S.P. Ayyar's reaction against the ills of the contemporary Indian society—enforced widowhood, religious orthodoxy, superstition and hypocrisy—must have brought him to the sphere of drama. He seeks to present men and things as he sees them and he also projects his own point of view. Ayyar thought that "by appealing to the feelings of chivalry, fair play and justice, enforced widowhood may finally disappear from Hindu society, though the reluctance to marry widows may continue for centuries more."[1] This reflects his zeal for social reform through his plays.

In his second play, *Sita's Choice* (1935), Ayyar deals with the problem of widow re-marriage. The play shows how a young widow finds fulfilment in her marriage with a reformist youth.

The play begins with the conversation between a wife and a husband in a small house in a village called Krishnagiri. Mangala. "a buxom matron of 42, with face and features expressing strength of character and a will to rule," (59) tells her husband Srinivas, "a man of 46, with the expression of an overgrown boy," (59) about the marriage of their daughter, Sita. She is prepared to give her daughter, Sita, in marriage to Vengu, a widower "for the paltry bridegroom price of five hundred rupees." (60) The husband is opposed to this marriage with "a consumptive-looking, prematurely aged man of 40, with all his hair gone grey." (71) The Act ends with the justification of the proposal by Mangala.

Act II begins with the news that Sita's marriage is already over and that her parents have incurred debt on this marriage. The parents realize their mistake of having performed the marriage of their daughter with a man who is already "wedded to a cruel disease."

Act III takes place after eight months of Sita's marriage. Vengu repents of his marriage with Sita. Andammal, his mother, justifies the marriage for two reasons. First, she wants to have an intelligent young daughter-in-law to help her in her old age Secondly, she says:

> Our family was about to die out. Our duty to our ancestors required that you should marry again, get children, and avert this catastrophe. (72)

These lines throw light on the selfishness of Andammal, the old woman.

Act IV deals with the evil days that befall the family of Srinivas after Sita's marriage. Srinivas informs his wife that he is involved in the embezzlement of funds to the tune of rupees 2,000/- from Ratnam & Co., and that the son of Ratnam has come to know about this. As such, he has no other option than to sell his house and the other plot. When Ratnam goes there to establish ownership on the house and the plot, Mangala argues cleverly and reaches a compromise with Ratnam. At this moment Vedaram, "a well-kept school master, aged 38" (73) enters the house with the sad news of the death of Vengu. Soon, Mangala goes upstairs in the hope of creating "a new world and a new heaven for ourselves, leaving the old world Vengus and concubines behind for ever." (85)

Act V begins with a new note with Srinivas's carefulness in spending money. Srinivas receives a letter from Rajagopal, his son-in law, about Sita's re-marriage. Though he becomes angry in the beginning, he is convinced by what Mangala has said and he resolves to go ahead with Sita's re-marriage.

In Act VI, the search for a suitable boy fructifies because Achyuth, a Brahmin who is employed in Persia, accepts the hand of Sita when he sees her. Sita also evinces keen interest in the re-marriage and the play ends with the family of Srinivas hoping to clear the debts and get back the house and the other plot.

Though the play runs into six Acts, it has a tautly-knit structure. The playwright has succeeded in planting firmly the theme of re-marriage through the play. Srinivas is opposed to the idea of re-marriage. But he is also convinced of it in the end. Act I deals primarily with the marriage of Sita with Vengu, a widower. Acts II, III and IV constitute one unit as they deal with the problems confronted by the family of Srinivas after Sita's marriage. Acts V and VI in a way end with a note of re-assurance and happiness in the family of Srinivas because of Sita's re-marriage. Each Act is interlinked with the other, thereby achieving coherence.

A.S.P. Ayyar is one of the social playwrights who have succeeded in using the language in keeping with the characters and situations in the play. Most of the times, his language is simple, racy, realistic and earthy. For example, in the very opening of the play, the conversation between the wife and the husband is simple and realistic:

> Mangala: I have solved the problem of our Sita's marriage.
> Srinivas: (eagerly) You don't mean to say so? Who is the boy?
> Mangala: Vengu of Sivapuram. (59)

Any common reader can follow the language here easily.

Some of the passages in the play are poetic. Now and then, Srinivas comes out like a poet. For example, in Act II of the play, he tells Mangala poetically about Sita's marriage with Vengu:

> My heart bleeds at the idea that our Sita is wedded to this man who was already wedded to this disease. (67)

The comments of Srinivas on Vengu's debts are poetic indeed:

> Few people without assets are without debts. Nature abhors a vacuum. If assets depart, debts are sure to take their place, just as they teach in our schools that the cold air replaces the hot one when it goes up. You ought to have known this. (68)

In this play, some lines acquire significance in a particular context. A sentence in the day-to-day conversation may not acquire any significance, but used by an actor on the stage, it gets added significance. For example, Srinivas tells Mangala:

> The wretched creatures rob their victims without mercy. (80)

Here, the context is that Srinivas has illegal contacts with women. As such, he knows how women exploit the men who approach them. Another example is the sentence uttered by Andammal,

> Why should the old suffer more than the young? (72)

If one knows the context, one can appreciate this better. The context is this: Vengu overhears the doctor saying that he (Vengu) will die soon. So he feels sorry because he will be making the life of Sita miserable. Just then, his mother goes to him and expresses her selfish motive thus. She feels that young persons are not justified in leading a happy life at the cost of the old people.

A.S.P. Ayyar makes a scathing attack on the double standards adopted by men. In practical life, the woman is judged by man's law, as though she were not a woman but a man. Ayyar's vituperation is against the criticism regarding the re-marriage of the young widows. As Mangala rightly observes,

> Alas, all our young men are only after money, and have no eyes for beauty or accomplishments in a poor girl. (65)

These lines reveal to us the materialistic concerns of the young men in India. Similarly, Mangala comments on the married men:

> When it is not man's duty even when married and living with his wife, to remain faithful to his wife! Oh, how can you reconcile these double standards? . . . When you people of forty-five and fifty feel the need for additional or alternative mates, how dare you blame a young girl of sixteen with her whole life before her, desiring a mate. (87-88)

Such passages throw light on how men indulge in double

standards.

As a playwright with a social purpose, A.S.P. Ayyar not only records the events from the contemporary Indian society but also reacts to them through his plays. In this play, he comes out with a fervent appeal for widow re-marriage. In the words of K.P.K Menon, "Mangala is the dramatist's mouthpiece. Her arguments in favour of widow re-marriage are obviously Ayyar's own.[2]

In the middle of the play, Mangala and Srinivas even argue thus:

> Mangala: Why should old widowers be allowed to re-marry a fourth or fifth time and a young virgin widow be forbidden a mate?
>
> Srinivas: I don't want to argue with you. Get this clearly into your head. I shall never allow Sita to marry again.
>
> Mangala: How can you prevent it? The laws allow her to re-marry.

This conversation between Srinivas and Mangala brings out the message of the playwright that a widow must be given a choice to re-marry just as any widower has. Thus, the play dramatizes an explicit thesis recommending social reform. It is a fervent plea for the noble cause of widow re-marriage.

NOTES

1. A.S.P. Ayyar, *The Slave of Ideas and Other Plays* (Madras: V. Ramaswamy Sastrulu and Sons, 1952), pp. 1-2.
2. K.P.K. Menon, *A.S.P. Ayyar* (Madras: Macmillan, 1980), p. 4.

The Poet as Dramatist: Nissim Ezekiel Interviewed

Nissim Ezekiel is a familiar name in world poetry. After establishing recognizable success as a poet, he turned to playwriting. He is one who has enriched the Indian drama in English with his five plays—*Nalini, Marriage Poem, The Sleepwalkers, Song of Deprivation* and *Who Needs No Introduction.*

Nalini, his first play, brings out the hollowness of the modern world by exposing the pretensions of the two advertising executives. *Marriage Poem,* his second play, presents the joys and sorrows of a married couple by contrasting the male satiation and female devotion. *The Sleepwalkers,* his third play, deals with self-deception employed by the sophisticated elite. *Song of Deprivation,* his fourth play, describes the plight of the modern man who is deprived of privacy in life. *Who needs No Introduction* his fifth play, is about a professional politician who addresses the youth in a seminar on young generation.

Though primarily a poet, Ezekiel has his own views on the art of drama. Given below is the transcript of the interview with him that took place in 1986.

PBR: What comments do you offer on the present scene of Indian writing in English in general and of Indian drama in English in particular?

NE: I shall confine myself to questions about Indian drama in English. There is very little of it and considerably less is worth staging and reading. All the same, I believe in its need, value and prospects. Sooner or later, it will attract talent on a large scale and produce notable results. To be objectively critical of it is not to discount it altogether but only to be realistic about its paucity and quality.

PBR: What reasons do you ascribe to the paucity of Indian drama in English? What future do you envisage for it?

NE: The reasons for its paucity are many and complex but I feel I need not list them. There was a paucity of journals in English till not many years ago. Today we have a magazine boom. Tomorrow we may have something similar in drama. The time has to be ripe for it. Our culture, in general, will feel the need for it. As stated earlier, I envisage a future for it not less worthy than that for poetry and fiction in English.

PBR: Do you subscribe to the idea that Indian drama in English suffers mostly from its competition with the regional theatre and the absence of live audience?

NE: Both the reasons mentioned in your question are valid, but things don't remain the same in contemporary societies. We should quietly work for the changes called for in our cultural situation, and hope for the best. Being merely discouraged is not of much use.

PBR: "If the Indian theatre is dead at all, it is dead because the days of great play-writing appear to have vanished." Do you agree with this?

NE: We may not get great play-writing, comparable to the world's greatest, but we are likely to get serious and interesting work. That would be enough to hope, for greatness may follow, when it is least expected. It may come as a surprise, through one outstanding figure, and that will lead to better performance by others in the field and by a whole generation of newcomers.

PBR: Can you specify the reasons that prompted a poet like you to play-writing?

NE: I became interested in the theatre through my association with E. Alkazi and his work in Bombay's Theatre

Group. Later, we formed the Theatre Unit. To write plays became at that time a dream for me and to some extent it is still a dream. More than fifteen years passed after my first five plays were written, and I regret the lapse but expect to make up for it before the end of the 80s.

PBR: It seems that almost all your plays are written during one period i.e. between 1968-69, and no play of yours is published after *Song of Deprivation*. How can you account for this sudden loss of interest in play-writing?

NE: I did not lose interest in play-writing but failed to be creative in the field for a variety of personal reasons. I cannot blame anyone or anything for the failure.

PBR: Are you influenced by any playwright—native or foreign—in your writing plays?

NE: I can sense no real influences in my plays, as I can in my poetry.

PBR: Among your plays which one do you consider the best and the true representative of your dramatic art?

NE: I have not yet written plays substantial enough to be considered in terms of bad, good, better, best and worst. Compared to the other three, *Nalini* and *Marriage Poem* I consider worth staging.

PBR: Have you any particular message to convey through your plays?

NE: No, I cannot find a specific "message" in my plays, but I feel there are ideas in them which add to their dramatic value.

PBR: Do you agree with the opinion that your plays are "mild satires" on modern life?

NE: There is a satiric element in the plays, undoubtedly whether the satire is mild or sharp, I cannot say (I should not!). I am certain only that there is more than satire, positive statements about life and human relationships, but not enough to add up to a "message."

PBR: Do you feel that you have created living characters in

your plays?

NE: Yes, I feel my characters are living, but I don't like to make claim for my work. It is for the critics, readers and audience to decide.

PBR: I personally feel that your drama is a female dominant one. Do you agree?

NE: If you mean that women are the dominant characters in my plays, I don't agree. But they are certainly as important as the men characters.

PBR: May I know your philosophy of life and its bearing on your plays?

NE: I don't make claims about a whole philosophy of life expressed in the plays. There are perceptions, views, ideas, reasonably integrated.

PBR: What, according to you, is your dramatic theory?

NE: I can't claim, again, to have a whole dramatic theory. I believe that plays are written for performance and not only for reading. Therefore, they must have a strong theatrical element, that is all. The interest of the audience must be sustained, not only by the dialogue but by the movements, the action, the events that happen within the plot or story.

PBR: Of various elements of drama like plot, character, dialogue etc. which element gains the prime of place in your opinion?

NE: I have not tried to give "prime of place" to any one element but to balance them all to the extent possible.

PBR: Have you witnessed any of your plays being staged? If so, what effect does it create on you and how far are you satisfied with its theatricality?

NE: Yes, I have witnessed *Nalini* and *Marriage Poem* more than once, *Who Needs No Introduction* and *The Sleepwalkers* once. I feel that their theatrical elements had not been fully exploited. The question of being "satisfied" never arises for me. I try to be as critical of my work as I am of other people's.

PBR: In its Marathi translation, *Marriage Poem* impressed

the audience while the English play failed to do so, but the reverse proved true in the case of *Nalini*. The play in its Marathi translation was less impressive than its English original on the stage. How can you possibly account for this?

NE: I can't account for the difference you mention, as I don't have enough evidence on the subject.

PBR: There is a criticism that you have employed "Indianized English" only for the comic purpose and to denigrate the Indians who use it but have not explored its dramatic possibilities fully. Do you agree?

NE: I use Indian English for comic as well as realistic purposes. As for exploring its dramatic possibilities fully, I certainly would not claim that I have done so. But "denigration" is always far from my mind. Those who are touchy about the use of Indian English in literature will of course be suspicious. There is little I can do about that. The important thing for me is that the use of Indian English by some characters should be vindicated by their reality. Such characters exist, and that's the way they speak.

PBR: Having identified yourself with the Indian sensibility long ago, why do you feel alienated now?

NE: I have never wholly identified myself with "the Indian sensibility" nor do I feel alienated from it now. I have always believed that I have a particular relationship with that sensibility, which is part of my normal life. No one would accept any alleged "identification" with it by me and the charge of alienation I consider at the other extreme of interpretation. I am related to, not identified with, not alienated from.

PBR: Does your Jewish background have any influence in shaping your literary career?

NE: I am sure my Jewish background has something to do with my life, ideas, career, etc., but cannot define that something easily. One day I may do so.

PBR: How far did your role as a critic help you in writing

plays?

NE: I have always believed that a critic should be as critical of his own life and work as of other people. To the extent that I have tried to practise that principle. The role of a critic has helped me in the writing of my plays.

PBR: In one of the interviews, you have stated that your dramatic work is an "extension" of yourself. How can you relate your play-writing with your poetry?

NE: Essentially, the same person is behind the plays as behind the poetry. If there are differences, the careful reader of both will discover and comment on them.

PBR: Do you intend to publish any Latter-day plays as you have published *Latter-day Psalms?*

NE: *Latter-Day Psalms* includes a series commenting on the Old Testament Psalms in the form of Psalms. Latter-Day does not mean, in this context, later than my poems. So the question does not arise. I certainly do intend to publish selections of poems written after *Latter-Day Psalms.*

PBR: Did you ever teach Indian drama in English? In your view, what role can a University teacher play in promoting Indian drama in English?

NE: I did a little bit of that during my last few years in the Bombay University's Department of English (I retired on 20 April '85). If a University teacher is capable of directing a play, he could choose an Indian play written in English, at least occasionally. He could also review and in general write about Indian drama in English on suitable occasions, do readings for AIR, and so on. There's plenty to do, always, in this as in other areas, if one has the will and the drive.

PBR: To your knowledge, is there any full-length study published on your plays?

NE: If by full-length you mean a book, then the answer is no. There have been a few articles, reviews and interview segments on the subject.

PBR: How do you view the research work going on on Indian drama in English? What advice do you offer to the young researchers in the field?

NE: Research workers in this area should know the odds. They should study the social and cultural context of the subject in addition to the texts. Once they begin doing that, they will come up with plenty of data and ideas, even if the actual body of relevant drama is small, They need, of course, a strong feeling for drama as theatre, the art of acting, stage designing and so on. I can only advise them not to lose interest because of real or alleged paucity of plays.

Minor Joys and Sorrows: Ezekiel's *Marriage Poem*

Marriage Poem[1] is "a one act tragi-comdey" that mirrors the "minor joys and sorrows"[2] of a married couple. Naresh and Mala are the couple in the play who "quarrel and compromise, love and hate and finally strike a helpless reconciliation with life itself."[3] The play depicts the dark and bright sides of the institution of marriage. The playwright examines "the paradox that is marriage and finds it to be more a comedy than a tragedy."[4] The play drives home the truth that happiness in married life rests largely on the mutual love and sympathy between a couple.

The play begins on a quiet domestic note. Mala, a housewife, "slightly emaciated but not unattractive," (59) is seen waiting for her husband to return from the office. She has set everything ready for the evening tea. Naresh, her husband, comes home "with a suitcase in his hand." (59) He does not offer any formal apology to his wife for his late-coming but straightaway engages himself in reading the letters on his table. This naturally irks his wife and she comes out with a complaint, "Are the bad moods reserved for me?" (60) Naresh places before her an invitation to dinner from the family of the Guhas. Mala, who has a strong dislike for Mrs. Guha, rejects the invitation and provokes Naresh with a sarcastic remark, "Mr. Guha's wife is a friend of my husband." (61) A minor skirmish follows between the couple but only to be rounded off with Mala's offering tea to her husband. After a few minutes of silence, Mala reminds her husband of the letter she has given him to post. Naresh apologetically rushes out to post it.

Mala who is left alone is visited by her "next-door neighbour" Mrs. Lall, "a middle-aged woman in a white sari." (63) She complains to Mrs. Lall about Naresh's indifference towards her. The extra-marital affairs of husbands in general become the subject of their discussion. When Mala asks her what she would do if her husband becomes attached to another woman, Mrs. Lall reacts to it sharply: "I would make a terrible fuss. I would harass my husband night and day till he gives her up." (65) This sounds to Mala a plausible solution to her own problem.

After a while, Naresh settles down to write some letters. Mala "tickles" him saying, "you're writing to one of your women." (67) Naresh gives a rebuff to her, "Yes, I'm writing to Indira Gandhi." (67) Mala, whose feelings are hurt, leaves the room in a huff.

In a dream-like sequence, Naresh, who is left alone, finds his girl-friend Leela before him. He transforms himself into a zealous lover and embraces her ecstatically. In the conversation that follows, he expresses his disgust with his wife and confesses his love for Leela. Soon his dream disappears, with the return of Mala into the room.

The couple resume the quarrel over the question of attending dinner at the Guhas. Mala bursts into tears and is cheered up soon by her husband with "gentle caresses" in his bid for reconciliation.

Malati and Ranjit, another couple, visit Mala and Naresh. Naresh invites them in warmly. Inspired by the presence of Malati, he speaks "the language of poetry" (74) which mystifies Mala.

When the Ranjits leave Naresh's room, Mala becomes critical of her husband's behaviour. The couple quarrel again. When the wife bursts into tears, Naresh "prepares to make love" to her in despair. The children's "loud, childish persistent knocking at the door" brings in the final reconciliation between them.

In this play, characters are distinctly types "for it is the situation that is central and dominant."[5] Mala in this play comes to us as typical fusion of the traditional and the modern woman. Like a traditional woman, she would like "to cling to her husband with increasing despair."[6] She wants to share her evening tea with her husband and even expects a word of appreciation from him. She does not brook the very mention of the names of other women by her husband. Like a typical Hindu bride, she is emotional and has no interests other than her husband and children. She wants to be pretty.

> Complacent at being fated,
> Never to be separated?[7]

Like a modern woman, Mala is very practical and bold. She seeks advice of Mrs. Lall, an elderly woman. She is frank in pointing out her husband's coldness in love. Naresh's sudden exuberance with Malati makes this modern woman say, "you never want to say anything to your wife. But when visitors come, you know how to talk. What long speeches!" (77) Finally, she wins her husband back through her unfaltering devotion, deep love and strong persuasion. She is in a way like Lavinia in *The Cocktail Party* who "works out her salvation with diligence."[8]

Naresh comes to us as a husband who, "tired of his wife, seeks escape and expression of his unfulfilled free self with other women."[9] He lives with his wife but adores Leela and enjoys the company of Malati. He simply believes that "genes" are responsible for his extra-marital behaviour. In his own words, "The genes are gods." (71) His explanation to Mala that "Our temperaments are very different" (79) is not cunning but serves as a camouflage to his inherent weakness.

Naresh is no hard-hearted villain but an erring human being, conscious of his own weakness. His confession to Leela— "I am the cause of my wife's suffering. I don't want to be the cause of your suffering too" (69—reveals this. He is caught in the crossfire of marital loyalty and romantic love. He is not strong enough to love completely either his wife or his girl-friend but withholds from both. In his cold manner to his wife, he is "seen in a role close to Sir Henry Harcourt Reilly of *The Cocktail Party*."[10]

Naresh looks upon marriage as a bondage. He values the freedom of an individual more than his filial duties. The poetic speech he makes in the presence of Malati reveals this fact. He says:

> I'm alone. It has taken me a long time to learn how to be alone. I've also learnt how to value the condition. The whole world is recreated when one achieves it. All art, poetry, music every thing that is true and beautiful is for the single man. Even Nature exists only when a man sees her alone. Only when he is alone does she undress for him. (74)

He finds in Leela a sort of emotional substitute to his wife. Leela is an image conjured up by him typifying all that is lacking in his relationship with Mala.

Malati and Ranjit are a happy couple in the play. They are well-adjusted and provide a good contrast to Mala and Naresh. They think differently yet they accommodate thought. Malati believes, "Husband and wife always think differently" (75) and she also finds comedy in it. She supports Naresh in his debate on vice and virtue and becomes his interpreter. The frustration of Mala and Naresh is contrasted with the mirthful spirit of Malati and Ranjit to reveal the fact that marriage is "More a comedy than a tragedy, more a poem than a dirge."[11]

Mrs. Lall is an interesting character in the play. She is a typical "next-door neighbour" found on the Indian scene. She is very genuine and sincere in her advice. She is a woman capable of making "a terrible fuss" if her husband runs after other women. The very thought of her husband's infidelity rouses her emotions and she becomes hysterical. She declares, "I wouldn't eat, and I would not allow him to eat. I would not sleep and I wouldn't allow him to sleep. I would behave like a mad woman. I would tear his hair. I would scratch my face and I would scratch his face." (65) Further, she is prepared to "quarrel with him in the streets," "spit" at the other woman and "take out a procession" and "shout slogans" against her husband. Her aggressiveness reminds us of the typical behaviour of any Indian housewife caught in such a predicament. Her hysterical utterances lend a touch of mock-seriousness to the play.

Leela, a girl-friend of Naresh, meets him only once a week. The fact that Naresh is a married man never upsets her. She is prepared to share his love with Mala. She says, "I'm happy when I'm with you. I'm happy to be loved by you." (69) She assures Naresh, "I'll always come back, whenever you need me." (80) Naresh who is unmoved by the kisses and caresses of his wife gets electrified in Leela's mere presence and becomes a passionate lover. Leela—real or fanciful—gives form to the romantic dreams of Naresh.

The setting of the play is quite in conformity with the mood of the characters. The scene of action is "a drab, middle-class drawing-dining room," fitted with "a mixture of modern and old fashioned" furniture. It has no curtains, no carpets and no flowers. Book cases, uncleared dining table, papers, files and books strewn on the writing desk give an effect of untidiness. "Flat, thin lighting from overhead bulbs" and the "large painting heavily overlaid with dust" suggest the absence of colour or cheerfulness in the life of the occupants of the house. The "untidy" room reflects their disturbed state of mind. The toys thrown about on a small mat indicate the presence of children. A "loud, childish persistent knocking at the door," (80) at the end of the play, makes not only the couple but also the audience feel the existence of children. By shifting the "spot light" from the couple to the mat on which the toys are spread, the playwright suggests their possible final reconciliation. The appearance of children is fraught with symbolic significance. They are the fruits of parents's love and the agents of harmony. The knock at the door is an awakening of their parental duty to children.

Music in this play, as in *Nalini*, excites the curiosity of the audience. The play begins with "pre-curtain music" and it continues till the end with intermittent rise and fall. It is heard softly in the background when the dialogue goes on and breaks out loudly at every pause.

The skirmishes between Mala and Naresh are beautifully intonated by the music. In the final scene, when Naresh sumbits himself to his wife's embrace, the music stops abruptly. In the silence that follows, the only sound that is heard is the children's knock at the door. The music begins again loudly. Thus, the musical crescendo gives to the play a growing forcefulness to which the audience can hardly fail to respond.

Ezekiel is successful in employing gestural language in this play. Gestures are significant movements of limbs of body which create an effect more than that of a dialogue. At the beginning of the play, Mala is seen "eating slices of bread which she dips into her cup of tea." (59) It is an effort on her part to conceal her despair or disappointment. She twists her face in annoyance as Naresh enters and smiles at him to appear quite normal. She "picks up a magazine" and "flips over its pages nervously" to relieve herself of the mental agony or tension.

A hypothetical question from Mala about her husband's loyalty transforms Mrs. Lall completely. Mrs. Lall is caught in the web of emotion. She "stands up briskly, utters half the words below standing, the rest walking up and down." (65) At the end of her rhetoric, she "sinks into a sofa in a state of collapse," "breathing heavily" and "avidly drinks a glass of water" offered by Mala. These gestures of Mrs. Lall are more powerful than her words in bringing about her real feelings to the fore. They reveal her disturbed state of mind.

The play is rich in aphoristic statements like, "Only his wife knows a man," (74) "The genes are Gods," (71) "Gods don't kiss," (71) "Husband and wife always think differently," (75) "Every woman is an understanding woman except your wife." (77) These aphorisms are woven into the texture of the play thereby intensifying its meaning.

The play has some exquisite touches of humour. Mala

asks Mrs. Lall whether her husband has any extra-marital affairs. Immediately Mrs. Lall replies, "My husband! My husband running after other women! They would run away from him. No, my poor husband is not that type." (64) This is genuinely humorous. Asked about what she is going to do with her husband if he is attached to another woman, Mrs. Lall replies, "I'll write to all the papers. I'll complain to the Home Minister. What is the use of being Home Minister if he can't guarantee the sanctity of the home?" (65)

Irony is one technique which Ezekiel employs in this play to make it powerful. The title itself is ironical because the play is about marriage where two people live together but do not know each other. It is with irony that Ezekiel peels layer after layer from a marriage that blisters. Ezekiel mocks at an institution that sanctions such loveless love-making, a marriage without understanding.

Another instance of irony is Mala's statement about her husband: "He is happy with me but he does not know it." (76) Moreover, her husband never does anything for her sake whereas she does many things for his sake. Mala tells her husband that she knows him better than he knows himself. Immediately, Naresh comments ironically: "It is sad that you should say so. Men run away from women who know them too well." (79) It is by employing the element of irony that Ezekiel makes his play admirably effective.

The end of the play may appear "theatrical and rather contrived"[12] but it serves a dramatic purpose. The play could have safely ended after Naresh makes love to Mala. At that point, Mala is blissfully happy for the first time in the play. The reappearance of Leela indicates that Naresh's reconciliation with Mala is not complete. He is much surprised to find Leela again before him and says, "You! I thought you would never come back." (80) The reappearance of Leela and his awakening to the children's knock at the door brings Naresh back to reality and makes his reunion with Mala final.

In the words of Fritz Blackwell, "*Marriage Poem* is an effective treatment of the familiar marriage-at-the menopause, not the woman's but the man's—and consequently the marriage's."[13] In a way, the play works out the condensed imagery of Ezekiel's poem "Marriage."

NOTES

1. Nissim Ezekiel, *Three Plays* (Calcutta: Writers Workshop, 1969).
2. Chetan Karnani, *Nissim Ezekiel* (New Delhi: Arnold Heinemann, 1974), p. 119.
3. Anisur Rahman, "Technique and Motif in Nissim Ezekiel's *Three Plays*." *Indian Writing in English*, ed. Krishna Nandan Sinha (New Delhi: Heritage, 1979), p. 57.
4. Murli Das Melwani, "Paucity of Indo-Anglian Drama," *Themes in Indo-Anglian Literature*, 2nd ed. (Bareilly: Prakash, 1977), p. 18.
5. Fritz Blackwell, "Four Plays of Nissim Ezekiel," *Journal of South Asian Literature*, Vol. XI, Nos. 3-4 (Spring-Summer 1976), p. 268.
6. H.M Williams, *Indo-Anglian Literature: 1800-1970: A Survey* (Madras: Orient Longman, 1976), p. 124.
7. Nissim Ezekiel, "Marriage," *The Unfinished Man*, 2nd ed. (Calcutta: Writers Workshop, 1965).
8. T.S. Eliot, *The Complete Poems and Plays of T.S. Eliot* (London: Faber and Faber, 1954), p. 411.
9. H.M. Williams, p. 124.
10. H.H. Anniah Gowda, "Nissim Ezekiel's Plays," *Literary Half-Yearly*, XIV, 1 (Jan. 1973), p. 14.
11. Murli Das Melwani, p. 18.
12. Chetan Karnani, p. 120.
13. Fritz Blackwell, p. 268.

The Hollowness of Middle-Class Society: *Nalini*

Nalini,[1] "a comedy in three Acts," is Ezekiel's first play. It exposes the hollowness and pretensions of contemporary society by its realistic portrayal of life around us. It mainly "explores the world of advertisement, to many the most glamorous and to others the most shallow of the westernized sections of the population."[2] The encounter of two successful modern advertising executives with a modest young painter becomes the central incident in the play. The playwright unmasks the vile tricks employed by the deceptive advertising agents and the bold resistance put forward by a genuine artist. Ezekiel's familiarity with the world of advertising, first as an art critic of *The Times of India*, and later as the manager of "Shilpi Advertising" helped him shape the play into a powerful satire.

The play has a tautly-knit structure with a good beginning, a good middle and a good ending. There are only three characters in the play. Yet they are all well-differentiated to meet the needs of the plot. The entire action is woven round one central figure Nalini. The play moves from reality to fantasy and again to reality. In the first Act, Nalini's painting becomes the subject of discussion between Bharat and Raj. In the second Act, Bharat's encounter with two Nalinis—one in fantasy and the other in reality—is presented. The third Act brings back Bharat and Raj to their own life-style. Thus the play ends where it began. By proceeding from reality to fantasy and back to reality the play exposes man's interest "in shadow rather than in substance."[3]

The play lives on dialogue. It opens with a "bit of brilliant and implicitly friendly dialogue"[4]:

Raj: Hello, am I disturbing you?
Bharat: You are.
Raj: I have a reason to. What are you doing at the moment?
Bharat: I am listening to music.
Raj: What are you doing, apart from listening to music?
Bharat: I am sitting still.
Raj: What are you doing, apart from sitting still?
Bharat: Pascal says that some of evil in the world would be much diminished if men could only learn to sit quietly in their rooms (sitting back and stretching out his legs) I am busy diminishing the sum of evil in the world. (9)

Here the dialogue creates a sense of nothingness because Bharat feels that by "sitting still" in his room, he can reduce the sum of evil in this world. This is also characterized by ease and informality that make the play powerful on the stage.

In the words of C. Paul Verghese, "the dialogue however, should be such that it does not draw attention to itself but to the speakers. The dialogue should be transparent medium of character."[5] In his dialogues, Ezekiel is successful in adapting the English language to reflect the idiom of the language of the characters in the play.

In Act II where Bharat encounters Nalini of his fantasy, the language is light, easy, racy and sparkling. But in his meeting with real Nalini in the same Act, the language is dense and has conversational weight. The following passages illustrate the point in hand. Act II opens with Nalini, "a dream character, smart, very pretty and possessing no talent for painting,"[6] greeting Bharat:

Nalini: (Sweetly, drawing it out) Hel-lo!
Bharat: Come in, come in. I was expecting you.
Nalini: What a lovely room this is. Did you do it up

yourself?

Bharat: (Modestly) Well, not entirely, I consulted a friend, I'm glad you like it. Won't you sit down?

Nalini: (Moving round the room appreciating various features of it. He follows her with eyes and body), I will in a moment. (Pause) So you're going to help me with the publicity for my exhibition? I am so grateful.

Bharat: Don't be grateful so early. I haven't done anything yet. (25-26)

Real Nalini, a genuine artist, meets Bharat and exposes his sham goals:

Bharat: I'm sincere enough to tell you now that I don't understand painting, least of all modern painting.

Nalini: And you spend your time and energy promoting art, helping artists. Why do you do it?

Bharat: I enjoy doing it. I like people, and it gives me a certain satisfaction to help them. Isn't that a good reason?

Nalini: Why choose art?

Bharat: What else can I choose? I can't do this kind of work in any field. I'm not that sort of man. I can't help to uplift masses, you know. (32-33)

This bit of dialogue reveals to us the insincerity of Bharat with regard to modern painting. It also dwells upon the real interest of Nalini in Art. Thus, the playwright has succeeded in using the right dialogue in keeping with the characters and situations.

In the words of Styan, a particular passage in a play in a particular context acquires conversational weight. This is quite true of this play. For example, in Act I, Bharat says that he would like to "emulate the saints." (10) Immediately Raj reacts to it and asks him about Angela. By knowing the context, one can appreciate the lines better. The context is that Raj would like to say that they cannot increase the sum of good in the world without doing some evil. Immediately Bharat points out that he would like to emulate the saints thereby showing his interest in the promotion of peace. But Raj recalls Bharat's affair with Angela, a typist. These lines acquire conversational weight when the context is properly understood. Thus, *Nalini* displays "considerable craftsmanship in the handling of pace, and witty, lively, realistic dialogue and tone."[7]

The play proves itself to be theatrically vital. The playwright employs certain audio-visual devices which make the play unforgetfully powerful on the stage. The scene setting, the voices, the music and the ring of the bell add to the theatrical effect of the play. In Act I, Bharat's attractive small room, neatly furnished with books, modern paintings, excellent furniture, beautiful lighting arrangement and soft classical music, is in agreement with the nature of romantic and a non-conformist gentleman, Bharat.

The shift in the mood of the characters is suggested through minor changes in the setting. In Act II, "a large flower vase" is put and light is "spotted down only at the centre" and the rest of the room is "in virtual darkness." It is in keeping with the jubilant mood of Bharat. The lighting arrangements make the dream contrivance possible in the play. In Act III, the "bowl of flowers" is removed and the large abstract painting is replaced by a mere conventional landscape. It suggests the sad aftermath of the crisis faced by Bharat.

The "Voices" in Act I draw the attention of the audience and even control their minds. Sometimes "optimistic," sometimes "pessimistic" and "idealistic," (20-21) they represent the hum and buzz of a city life. They may even be the voices of conscience of Bharat and Raj.

Ezekiel employs music to intensify the effect of the play. In Act I, "soft," "quiet", "classical" music is heard. It rises sometimes, and falls at the other, thereby having its gripping effect on the audience. When the dialogue goes on, the music is lowered and the short silence between the dialogue is filled with a rise in the music. In Act II, Jazz is heard. It has snob value attached to it. In Act III, no music is heard at the beginning but later Bharat switches on the gramophone which pours out the music. It suggests the characters getting back into their world of make-believe.

Ezekiel makes an effective use of the bell. Every scene begins with the ring of a bell, a modern urban gadget. The ring of the bell in the play is associated with the entry of a character on the stage. While Raj and Nalini of Bharat's fantasy make their entry with "a ring" of the bell, the real Nalini enters only with a "knock" at the door. In Act III, the ring of the bell brings Nalini of fantasy to Bharat and Raj. They encircle her and bawl out lovely rhythms in mad ecstasy. When she leaves them, they wish for the return of the real Nalini. They order the ring of the bell and it rings but Nalini never comes back. Again the bell rings violently and they feel terribly "upset" and insecure. They want the bell to be rung "properly, sedately and decorously." (53) Towards the end of the play, it goes beyond human control and becomes a "shattering roar." The gentle ring of the bell in the beginning and its blasting in the end signify the demolition of egoism and hollowness of the two advertising executives.

All these—the setting, the play of music and the ringing of the bell—provide enough backdrop for "an exposure of hollow, morbid, hypocritical city man."[6]

Wit is one element that makes *Nalini* strikingly appealing. Ezekiel has clothed all the three Acts of the play with a profusion of wit. For example, at the very opening of the play, Bharat says, "Men are cynical about women only in the presence of men." (18) Even in Act II, this witty vein of Bharat continues when he says, "I can't understand art but I understand artist. I could understand you if you gave a chance. I understand women." (38) In Act III, he says: "We think too well of ourselves. We are too comfortable. When we look into the mirror we see shining examples of the successful, modern young executive." (46) Thus, the playwright succeeds in charming the reader with the aid of wit.

Ezekiel uses satire as a powerful weapon thereby presenting a chillingly realistic picture of contemporary India. He satirizes artists and their art. In Act I, Raj comments satirically on paintings in general and Nalini's paintings in particular: "They are paintings, canvasses with colour on them, plenty of colour in various forms. They don't represent any thing. I guess, they are just paintings." (11) Even Bharat becomes critical of the artists who resort to cheap tactics to promote their art. They will "invite some big shot to open the exhibition. He'll make a speech praising your paintings. You'll arrange to have him garlanded. You'll socialize with the journalists who attend." (31) These lines of Raj and Bharat present a gloomy picture of the world of art.

Ezekiel assails the Indians who go abroad and come back without enriching their minds. Raj draws our attention to this aspect of the matter when he says, "You could go abroad and come back . . . you need not learn anything abroad. Just go and come back." (13) The playwright's sarcastic attitude is directed towards the modern Indian society which he holds to ridicule thus: "We are not slaves of caste. We are not superstitious. . . . We are not communalistic, provincial or parochial. . . . It is good that we are not what we are not. . . . Are we Indians?" (16) The same satiric vein continues even in Act II where Nalini says: "The Indian city is as Indian as the Indian village. I live in this city. . . . I want to interpret the atrocious, physical and moral squalor of our city." (32)

Thus, the playwright lashes out contemporary Indian urban society bringing about most effectively its squalor, anguish and misery.

To conclude, we may say that *Nalini* is a three-Act comedy which explores real and imaginary relationships. It is about Bharat and Raj, the advertising executives, who encounter Nalini, the painter, and realize their follies. The playwright uses dialogue in consonance with the situation and the characters. He employs certain theatrical devices which make the play effective on the stage. His use of dramatic devices like parallels and contrasts makes the play strikingly original. To put it in a nutshell, he sets out to hold a mirror to the hollowness of the urban middle class in India.

NOTES

1. Nissim Ezekiel, *Three Plays* (Calcutta: Writers Workshop, 1969).
2. Eunice de Souza, "Some Recent Indian Plays in English," *Perspectives on Indian Drama in English*, ed. M.K. Naik, S. Mokashi-Punekar (Madras: Oxford University Press, 1977), p. 157.
3. Chetan Karnani, *Nissim Ezekiel* (New Delhi: Arnold Heinemann, 1974), p. 118.
4. Rajiv Taranath, "Ezekiel's *Nalini*," *Indian Drama*, ed. H.H. Anniah Gowda (Mysore: University of Mysore, 1974), p. 119.
5. C. Paul Verghese, *Problems of Indian Creative Writer in English* (Bombay: Somaiya, 1971), p. 172.
6. H.M. Williams, *Indo-Anglian Literature 1800-1970: A Survey* (Bangalore: Orient Longman, 1976), p. 124.
7. Eunice de Souza, p. 158.
8. Anisur Rahman, "Techniques and Motif in Nissim Ezekiel's *Three plays*," *Indian Writing in English*, ed. Krishna Nandan Sinha (New Delhi: Heritage, 1979), p. 57.

Reflections on Asif Currimbhoy's Plays

Asif Currimbhoy is one contemporary Indian playwright in English who has created true drama by bringing life to the theatre and the theatre of life. Among the modern Indian playwrights, none has the international reputation as Asif Currimbhoy whose plays have been staged by dramatic groups of American Universities, repertory companies and the off-Broadway theatre. He got his start in 1965 when, after nearly fifteen years of writing without ever seeing a single play of his produced in India, the University of Michigan staged his *Goa*. Three years later it was produced at the Martinique Theatre on Broadway and 34th Street. The Theatre Company in Boston exhibited *The Hungry Ones*, and others—La Mama and the British Drama League—staged *The Dumb Dancer* with Kathakali dancers. *The Doldrummers*, his most powerful play, was successfully staged at Actors's Studios. As Faubion Bowers rightly observes: "Asif Currimbhoy has been India's first authentic voice in the theatre."

A Khoja Muslim, born in Bombay on August 15, 1928, Asif Currimbhoy hails from a family of industrialists who were awarded the title of baronetcy by the British government for their distinction in the field of industry. His father was a liberal-minded intellectual and his mother was a veteran social worker. Their distinguished intellectual concerns and outstanding commercial enterprise deeply touched the mental proclivities of Asif Currimbhoy in his teenage years. He was brought up in an environment of new ebullient ideas which in his later life formed an integral part of his temperament. He studied in St. Xavier's High School, Bombay, which exposed him to the English language and to some extent to the Western culture. After schooling in India, he studied at Wisconsin University before graduating from the University of California in Economics in 1950. As a University student, he loved and admired Shakespeare, witnessed numerous dramatic productions and was quite alive to the various trends in drama in the U.S.A. This must have gone a long way in shaping him as "a man of the theatre."

Asif Currimbhoy's literary interest was to a certain extent stimulated by his wife, Suraiya, whom he married soon after he returned to India. In a letter to Subhas Saha of Calcutta, he wrote: "I doubt if I would ever have been a writer were it not for my wife who gave me stability and sanity through home and love." Some of the characteristic features of his drama—the most recognizable sincerity, interest in society—show the extent to which the wife has influenced the husband in the art of drama. Obviously, the wife feels satisfied with her husband's literary performance when she calls her husband "a Karmayogi."

The offices Asif Currimbhoy held gave him an opportunity to see new places and meet all kinds of people. This provided him with the necessary milieu for his plays. His first assignment in New India Assurance Company was in Paris in 1954. He had the opportunity of acquainting himself with the French sophistication and culture. He soon left the New India Assurance Company and joined the Burmah Shell in India. As a marketing executive, he toured throughout India and acquainted himself with different locales and various problems of the people. In an interview to *Enact*, he says:

> The place had always had a considerable fascination for me and dialogues always appealed to me especially when they incorporated a feeling of diverse opinion.

From this, it is clear that Currimbhoy is a keen observer of people, particularly of their mode of expression.

All these influences have left their unmistakable impress

on the dramatic career of Asif Currimbhoy. Like Marlowe, Jonson, Greene, Marston, Dekker, Heywood, Shakespeare, and Beaumont and Fletcher, he began writing plays in his twenties. He chose to write for the theatre because he thought that this was the art form which allowed him most to show the complexity of the society he lived in. He entertained independent thinking, chose controversial themes, embodied them in arresting dialogue and constructed and resolved plots in an unconventional way.

Currimbhoy is a prolific playwright. He has taken unusual themes from contemporary Indian society and woven them into the plays of artistic excellence. As Peter Nazareth rightly observes, "Asif Currimbhoy interweaves the public event with the private to create exciting drama which asks moral questions about humanity in the cataclysmic period of decolonization." Not only does he record the events like the invasion of Goa *(Goa),* the flight of the Dalai Lama *(Om Mane Padme Hum!),* the assassination of Mahatma Gandhi *(An Experiment with Truth),* the famine in Maharashtra *(The Miracle Seed),* the visit of the beatniks to India *(The Hungry Ones),* the political situation in Gujarat *(The Dissident MLA),* and the Kathakali dance of Kerala (*The Dumb Dancer*), but passes "commentaries, consciously or otherwise" on them.

Within a span of fifteen years, Currimbhoy has written as many as thirty plays. He gathers his material mostly from a distinctly Indian experience and weaves various threads into it from the myths of yore as well as from the contemporary society. He has attempted almost every genre—comedy, tragedy, farce, melodrama, history and fantasy. His major plays may be divided thematically into various categories. His *Inquilab* (1970), *The Refugee* (1971) and *Sonar Bangla* (1972) may be called the Bengal trilogy in as much as they concern themselves with Bengal and its problems at different points of time. The romantic plays—*The Tourist Mecca* (1959), *The Doldrummers* (1960), *Darjeeling Tea* (1971) and *This Alien . . . Native Land* (1975)—deal with the plight of aliens and Anglo-Indians. They meet with a great success in the crafty coalescing of reality and reverie, and in the skilful use of the motif of sex as a theatrical strategy. The political plays—*Goa* (1964), *An Experiment with Truth* (1969), and *Om Mane Padme Hum*! (1972)—deal with some crucial political events that affected the body politic of India. The social plays—*Thorns on a Canvas* (1962), *The Hungry Ones* (1965), *The Miracle Seed* (1973) and *The Dissident MLA* (1974)—concern themselves with a realistic presentation of social problems.

Currimbhoy's achievement as a dramatist is marked by his impressive contribution to Indian drama in English. In the first place he presents life as it is, not as something it should be, the age-old practice of Indian classical theatre. He breathes an air of realism into his plays by making the setting, incident, character and dialogue contemporary with the times. Nevertheless he is not a literal-minded transcriber of mere facts. His plays are genuinely a microcosm of Indian life with their predilections, delusions, fantasies and their inveterate capacity to live in the past. Thus there is, in his plays, an interplay of realism and fantasy which gives them the unity and universality of great art.

Currimbhoy's plays may rightly be considered pieces of theatre "par excellence." He experiments with a variety of theatrical techniques to create visual and auditory images thereby producing the desired dramatic effect on the stage. By employing a variety of theatrical devices—quick shift of scenes, play within the play, dual scenes, chorus, chants, shadow cut-outs, pantomime, blackout, choreography—he tries to control the movements of the play and its impact on the audience. The pantomime in *The Hungry Ones*, the dance play of "the slaughter of Duryodhana" in *The Dumb Dancer*, the shadow cut-outs in *This Alien . . . Native Land* and the "Patio" walk in *Goa* produce tremendous visual effects which makes these plays more accessible physically to the audience.

Like Arnold Wesker, Currimbhoy is a playwright with a social purpose. His purpose is to provoke thought rather than to persuade the audience to adopt a specific plan of action. By presenting an aspect of life, he wants to import to them some of the enthusiasm he has for life. He has succeeded in writing a play which reconciles moving exploration of credible human situations with a desire to convey a message. In *Goa*, within the framework of a story centring round the rape of a Goan girl by an Indian boy, the dramatist makes it abundantly clear that though India takes over Goa, no one wins in view of the acute suffering and disintegration that set in among the Goans. The underlying thought of *The Hungry Ones* is that love and hunger stand out even in an environment of violence and looting. Thus in a Currimbhoy play, the long-held view of the theatre as ideal entertainment gives way to an understanding of the necessity of art as a contributing factor in the search for insight and to an understanding of man's essential role in discovering values which can represent his dignity.

Though Currimbhoy's plays are freighted with a message, they are primarily works of art. His plays are meant for the stage and they demonstrate his fine sense of the theatre and his skill as a dramatist. More than any contemporary Indian dramatist in English, he brilliantly succeeds in projecting an "image of the times." While his vigorous imaginative grasp of the pageant of life is reinforced by a dramatic use of colloquial idiom and imagery, his control of dramatic form makes his plays artistic and universal. He works his satire into the character, and the character into the plot ingeniously. His relentlessness is born out of his intellectual uprightness as well as of his artistic integrity.

Currimbhoy's plays are a product of his abiding faith in the efficacy of love and compassion. In fact, his whole approach to the drama is conditioned by his vision of life that love and compassion alone matter and that they serve as panacea to the ills of society. This philosophical basis can be recognized in the titles of his plays and in the kind of people he presents. His plays spring from his belief that in spite of endless arson and hopelessness, there is scope for values like love, peace and understanding. What he seeks to convey through his plays is that man should search for some meaning in life and the haven of security may rest in his faith in basic humanity and love. In his most representative play *The Hungry Ones*, the protagonist asks the American visitors to India to identify themselves with the hungry Indian:

> So you want to become
> one of us, stranger,
> a hungry one,
> then learn, stranger learn . . .
> HUNGER.

Small wonder, therefore, if this Indian dramatist writing in English has attained international reputation. His plays received critical attention even from the well-established western creative writers and critics. Struck by the boldness and imagination of Asif Currimbhoy's work, Arthur Miller calls him "a forceful playwright." Jeremy Brooks, Literary Manager, Royal Shakespeare Company, records: "There is a considerable admiration in England, and in this Company in particular, for the work of the Indian playwright Asif Currimbhoy." While the famous British novelist and playwright Graham Greene calls Asif Currimbhoy's *Goa* "a most remarkable piece of work," Rone Eyers acclaims it as "a masterful and an exciting theatrical event." Distinguished by careful craftsmanship and sensitively theatrical instinct, the plays of Asif Currimbhoy admirably illustrate the sophisticated artistry of contemporary Indian drama in English and they certainly deserve to be more widely read and produced both at home and overseas.

The Clock Symbol in Asif Currimbhoy's *The Clock*

The Clock is, in a sense, unique among not only Currimbhoy's plays but also the Indian plays in English. It is "a straight-run One Act Play with one scene and one actor." Though it is a one-man show, variations are introduced by the sound of voices of the characters on the stage who are audible but not visible. The one object which remains visible to the audience is a big clock, the sound of which serves as an undertone to the play. The scene of action is a shabby room with a radio, a telephone and a few books.

Henry, a man "about 45 years old with a very tired look about him,"[1] enters the room with a briefcase in his hand. He tells his wife that life is "a one way street with neat little blocks sliced up in years. All chronologically numbered if not in multiple progression." (90) He is in a dejected mood. As he could not promote the sales and could not raise up to the expectations of the boss, he has decided to resign his job. Moreover, as an individualist, he finds it very difficult to get along with his boss:

> All I want out of life is the right to live as I choose. Is that asking for too much? I don't want to be bullied and I don't want to play second fiddle. Somehow it's always been a fight because I happened to be the underdog every time . . . and now I'm tired. (94)

It is but natural that an individualist like Henry is subjected to a lot of agony.

After a while Joe, an old neighbour of Henry, enquires of the latter's family condition. Like Joe, Henry too would like to go to another town with better prospects. Soon, Henry receives a letter from a business broker who has offered to buy a large contract from him at net rates. He feels that his problems will be solved to some extent. His wife asks him to get back his letter of resignation.

After a while, the first gong of midnight is heard. Henry turns around desperately towards the clock. On his face is found a terrible expression of anger and frustration. With a savage cry, he picks up a stick and smashes the wall clock. He flings himself on the chair with his head in his hands. The tick-tock of "the dead clock" continues.

The prevalence of tension is one feature that holds our attention in this play. Like the characters in Chekhov's plays, a sense of tension grows up in Henry, the protagonist of *The Clock.* He is in conflict with the boss who has asked him to boost up sales. He finds it very difficult to do so because there is a lot of competition in the world of business. As he himself puts it, he is an individualist and does not like any interference by his boss. Moreover, Mary, his wife, does not allow him to leave for a new place where he can prosper. He tells Joe about his wife Mary who is very particular "to make more and more money," (99) although there is no scope for making huge profits in small business. Besides this, the wife does not like the idea of moving out:

> You know what women are; they feel insecure in new surroundings. And then there is the kid's schooling and new house and neighbourhood and a whole lot of things to rearrange. She keeps talking about roots all the time. Like we were trees or something. (101)

Added to this, there is a continuous "voice of quarrelling followed by a bawl." (92)

The Clock a is symbolic play. The clock symbolizes the predicament of a salesman in the world of business. The "tick-tock'' of the clock symbolizes the ''lub-dub'' of the heart of the salesman. Just as the hands of the clock rotate continuously, the salesman too should go round from one place to another. The wind given to the clock makes it work properly. Similarly there must be a godhead to encourage the salesman and to make him have a smooth sail. The chiming of the clock is similar to that of the target which the salesman is supposed to achieve.

The play is highly theatrical. The playwright employs both the theatrical and dramatic devices to make the play powerful on the stage. ''Only a part of the scene is visible at any one time depending on the diameter and focus of the light as it follows the main actor.'' (88) The dream sequence, the shadow of Mary, the voices produced by Joe and the Doctor remind the audience constantly and explicitly that they are in a theatre. The stage setting also serves as a means of providing background material for the audience. The playwright has used a variety of dramatic devices like soliloquy (94, 99, 104, 108 and 114) and Irony. (95) Here is an instance of irony:

> Henry: Ever since I quit college without getting a degree I've been quitting everything else without ever finishing the job. (95)

Just as Chekhov has made the telling use of sounds in *Uncle Vanya,* Asif Currimbhoy has used sounds to create and enhance a melancholy atmosphere in the play. For example, the clicking of the heels of Mary, the bawl of children, the ring of the door bell, the chiming of the clock, the clutches on the belly, the gulp of beer, and smoking of cigarettes create the melancholy atmosphere in the play.

NOTES

1. Asif Currimbhoy, *The Tourist Mecca* and *The Clock* (Bombay: Asia, 1961), p. 88.

The Theatrical Representation of History: Girish Karnad's *Tughlaq*

> True drama is created by bringing life to the theatre and the theatre to life. . . . Good drama must be equally satisfying on each level . . . as character and action and life, on the one hand, and the highly conventional art of the theatre, on the other. And unless the dramatist works like an organist playing on two keyboards at once, the audience cannot respond as it wishes to respond.[1]

Girish Karnad is a contemporary Indian playwright who has created true drama in his play *Tughlaq*[2] in the Priestleyan sense. He explores the paradox of Muhammad Tughlaq, the idealistic Sultan of Delhi whose reign is considered to be one of the most spectacular failures in Indian history. *Tughlaq* is not an ordinary chronicle play but a very imaginative reconstruction of some of the most significant events in the life of a great king who is seen not only in India but also in the contemporary world. The theme of the play is from Indian history yet the treatment of it is not historical but highly political. In this play, politics is ingeniously linked with people, religion and history.

In the very opening of the play, an old man and a young man discuss the political situation in the country. In their discussion, they bring about a sharp contrast between the present administration of Tughlaq and the administration of the past Sultans. Again in scene vii, one finds a discussion on the importance of politics in day-to-day life, Aziz, a washerman turned politician, says: "Only a few months in Delhi and I have discovered a whole new world—politics! My dear fellow, that's where our future is—politics! It's a beautiful world—wealth, success, position, power—and yet it's full of brainless people, people with not an idea in their head." (50) In scene xi too, "Crowds of citizens" discuss among themselves how the rulers went to save the common men who are ridden by starvation, dirt, disease, impatience, famine and a number of other ills. One comes to know from this how politics is used to promote the self-interest of the leaders but not the welfare of people.

In this powerful play, politics is deftly linked with religion. In scene iii, one finds the Revered Sheikh Imam, aligning himself with politics. He accepts the plea of the Sultan to serve as his envoy and dissuade Ain-ul-Mulk of Avadh from the folly of turning against the Sultan. A platoon of heavily armed soldiers follows him while he is doing the job of an emissary. The Sultan has managed to kill Imam in such a way that nobody would suspect him. Here the religious leader becomes a prey to the dirty political game of Tughlaq. Prayer, which is deeply allied to religion, is used for murder in the play. Prayer halls are being polluted with these discussions on politics. Tughlaq kills his father while he offers prayers. Chieftains are worried about the deft political intrigue practised by Tughlaq on Imam. Shihab, one of the Amirs, cries out thus: "Is it so reprehensible to worry about people? Is it a crime to speak out for oneself and one's family? What politics did Sheikh Imam-ud-din indulge in? That he was open, frank and honest?" (32) He also adds how religious leaders like Haidari and Hood are in prison. These events clearly reveal to us how religion is made use of by the politicians for their selfish ends.

Besides religion, history is cleverly linked with politics in this play. Barani, a historian, is asked to give a practical remedy for "the honey comb of diseases" (55) like the uprising of the Deccan, the declaration of independence by Habar

Ehasanshah. The historian wonders why the Sultan who has faith in love, peace and God has now grown pessimistic about the future. The playwright links history with politics by making the historian align himself with the political activity of the Sultan. As U.R. Anantha Murthy observes, "The whole play is structured on these opposites of the ideal and the real, the divine aspirations and the deft intrigue." (ix) In the main plot, Tughlaq appears to be idealistic but instead he practises selfish political game. The scenes are so juxtaposed that one is not allowed to be either carried by one's hatred towards Tughlaq for his master tactics or by one's sympathy or admiration for his idealism.

Karnad displays great talent in the delineation of the character of Tughlaq. Throughout the play, one finds elements of dualism in the character of Tughlaq. As an idealist, he aims at the welfare of his people; but he practises hypocrisy by employing a Hindu officer to watch the Muslim soldiers and vice versa. As a pious Muslim, he prescribes the customs of prayer five times a day, but as a crafty politician, he indulges in deft intrigue. He kills his father, his brother and Shihab while they are at prayer. He is highly resourceful and imaginative because he can solve easily "the most famous problem" in chess which was not solved by experts like al-Adli and as-Sarakhi. Barani rightly says: "You are a learned man, your Majesty, you are known the world over for your knowledge of philosophy and poetry. History is not made only in statecraft; its lasting results are produced in thc ranks of learned man." (55) In the words of his own stepmother, Tughlaq is "an intelligent boy and he works so hard for the people. He doesn't even go to bed these days." (17) The playwright has succeeded in presenting the conflict in the mind of Tughlaq.

Karnad's handling of dialogue in the play is quite effective. He has chosen English to reflect the idiom of the language of character. A Karnad sentence often performs two or three functions at once. It sheds light on the character speaking, on the character spoken about and it furthers the plot. It almost functions ironically in conveying to the audience a meaning different from that conveyed to the character. The following lines illustrate the point:

> Muhammad: No one can go far on his knees. I have a long way to go. I can't afford to crawl—I have to gallop.
>
> Imam-ud-din: And you will do it without the Koran to guide you? Beware, Sultan, you are trying to become another God. It's sin worse than parricide. (21)

This passage throws light on the aspirations of Tughlaq to the fame of becoming a universal conqueror. He would not like to crawl but would like to gallop. In the pursuit of his ambition, he may even ignore the tenets of the holy Koran. An astute politician as he is, he feels that he has not yet made considerable advance in the realm of politics. Naturally, the dialogue here gives an insight into the political theme of the play and the playwright's power to handle this theme. The dialogue furthers the theme of the political gambit of Tughlaq.

A snatch of a phrase caught in everyday conversation may mean little. Used by an actor on the stage, it can assume general and typical qualities. In the words of Styan, "the context into which it is put can make it pull more than its conversational weight, no matter how simple the words."[2] For example, Tughlaq, who has ingeniously manoeuvred to bring about the death of Imam-ud-din in the battlefield, declares a day of mourning in honour of the Sheikh and says: "When men like him die, it's a sin to be alive." (28) These words acquire theatrical vitality easily. Equally interesting and powerful is the conversation between Tughlaq and Shihab. Tughlaq says: "It's a question of confidence. A question of trust! The other day I heard that in China they have paper currency—paper, mind you—and yet it works because the people accept it." (39)

Tughlaq is notable for its poetic value. Tughlaq comes to us as a poet when he speaks of his interest in the Greeks. He says: "Don't I know it? I still remember the days when I read the Greeks—Sukrat who took poison so he could give the world the drink of gods, Aflatoon who condemned poets and wrote incomparably beautiful poetry himself—and I can still feel the thrill with which I found a new world, a world I had not found in the Arabs or even the Koran." (21) Here poetry has made the play precise not only for the actor to work with but also for the audience to react to. The poetry here expresses and defines patterns of thought and feeling otherwise inexpressible and indefinable.

Sometimes language in the play is simple, easy and precise. The language of the people from the lower strata of life, like servants and soldiers, is direct, simple and powerful. The following is a case in point:

> Old Man: God, what's this country coming to!
> Young Man: What are you worried about, grandfather? The country's in perfectly safe hands—safer than any you've seen before.
> Old Man: I don't know. I've been alive a long time, seen many Sultans, but I never thought I would live to see a thing like this. (1)

Through such careful choice of characters and situations, Karnad endeavours to make his dialogue realistic, immediate, precise and highly effective.

Silences and pauses mark a silent interplay of conscious and unconscious motivation. One is naturally reminded of *The Dumb Waiter* of Pinter. In scene iii, in the encounter between Tughlaq and Iman-ud-din, one finds a long silence in the middle of the dialogue. (22) Tughlaq tells Imam-ud-din that people will greet him as a spy in the market place. He also praises him that as a great saint, the Sheikh has risked his life speaking out against the Sultan. The long silence there tells us that Tughlaq is a crook and is interested in killing Imam. Again, in the conversation between Tughlaq and his stepmother, (27) Tughlaq pauses for a while when he actually describes the death of Imam-ud-din. This reflects the negative side of Tughlaq. One finds similar pauses in the conversation between Sheikh and Shihab. These silences and pauses reinforce the meaning of the play.

Tughlaq is rightly considered a piece of theatre "par excellence." Karnad experiments with a variety of theatrical techniques to create visual and auditory images, thereby producing the desired dramatic effect on the stage. By employing a variety of theatrical devices—spectacle, quick shift of scenes, blackout—he tries to control the movement of the play and its impact on the audience. Spectacle refers to all the visual aspects of production, scenery, lighting, costume, make-up and the business and the movement of the actors. In the very beginning of the play, the public announcer announces the judgement of the Chief Justice in favour of Vishnu Prasad followed by a loud discussion among a large number of people. The very appearance of Tughlaq in his striking costume adds a lot to the element of spectacle in the play.

The announcement pertaining to the arrival of Sheikh Imam-ud-din enhances the visual appeal of the play. Muezzin's call for prayer, the marching of the Amirs towards the throne of Tughlaq, the announcements made by the announcer about the shifting of capital from Delhi to Daulatabad, the call for the banning of prayer and the revival of it, the play of music and the anguish expressed by the common masses during the shift of the capital, are some of the elements of spectacle in *Tughlaq* that have come to assume an organic psychological role in the theatre that reinforces the meaning of the play.

There are 13 scenes in the play which runs into 86 pages. The scene of action is almost suddenly shifted from the yard in front of the Chief Court of Justice to a room in the palace, then to the yard in front of the Big Mosque, again to the palace, then to a house in Delhi and then to the palace again. It shifts to a camp on the Delhi-Daulatabad road. Suddenly it goes to the fort in Daulatabad, to a hide-out in the hills, then to the palace, and then to a plain outside the fort of Daulatabad, and back to the palace. The playwright presents the following sequences to throw light upon the complex personality of the Sultan: The affair of Aziz and Adam, Tughlaq's attempt to levy heavy taxes on the poor farmers, his orders to change the capital from Delhi to Daulatabad, the futile conspiracy of the disgruntled Amirs to kill the Sultan while at prayer; his cruel punishment of his stepmother because she was responsible for the killing of Vizier Nazib; Aziz's impersonation of the invitee Caliph Ghiyas and its consequences; and finally the fall of the Sultan. As these episodes follow each other on the stage, they make us focus our attention on Tughlaq as a complex character. Moreover, the sudden shifting of the scenes makes the spectator move forward and backward. The audience is constantly and explicitly reminded that it is in a theatre while the play is made as accessible as possible.

Karnad deftly uses a few dramatic techniques which add much to his artistry. Irony is one technique which he employs to make his play highly theatrical. It is not merely situational but also verbal. The manner in which prayer is sought to be used as an instrument of murder against the very man who has made prayers compulsory in the state, and the role played by Aziz are examples of the irony of situation. Again Aazam and his death, Ghiyasuddin's preferring "the bloody streets" to the palace are other examples of situational irony. The beautiful bodies which are eaten up by corruption are stuffed with straw and hung on the poles. Tughlaq asks Barani not to cover the dead body of Shihab because he wants his people to see the wounds.

A few instances of verbal irony. The past Sultans of Delhi could not bear the weight of their crown. They could not leave it aside. So they died senile in their youth or they were murdered. Barani, a historian, is interested in playing chess with the shadows of the dead. The prayers offered by Tughlaq are ridden with disease and his sins have become shadows that entwine round his feet. It is ironical that Tughlaq and the Sheikh look alike but they do not think alike.

Symbolism is another technique that Karnad employs to make his play powerful on the stage. One finds four major symbols in the play. They are prayer, sleep, the game of chess and the rose. At the micro level, prayer symbolizes the religious idealism of Tughlaq. At the macro level, it connects man's unconscious need for divine protection and guidance in an hour of anguish. In the beginning prayer is made compulsory but later it is banned for a few years and again it is revived. It is reduced to a mockery when the Sultan's life is threatened at the time of prayer. "Sleep" on one level represents the need for rest in man's life. At the macro level it becomes symbolic of peace which eludes man often. The rose is a symbol of the aesthetic and poetic susceptibilities of Tughlaq. It later on becomes a symbol of the withering away of all the dreams and the ideals of Tughlaq. At the macro level, the game of chess is an ordinary game which is popular in India. It also symbolizes a political game in which the most intelligent and clever politician is checkmated by an ordinary washerman. Through this symbolist technique, the playwright has succeeded in creating the right political atmosphere. Thus *Tughlaq* emerges as one of the significant plays in the Indian theatre today.

NOTES

1. J.B. Priestley, *The Art of the Dramatist* (London: Heinemann, 1957).
2. Girish Karnad, *Tughlaq* (Delhi: Oxford University Press, 1972).
3. J.L. Styan, *The Elements of Drama* (Cambridge: Cambridge University Press, 1967), p. 11.

The Novelist as a Short-Story Writer: Manohar Malgonkar

Manohar Malgonkar turned to short-story writing after writing novels. His short stories appeared in three volumes—*A Toast in Warm Wine* (1974), *Bombay Beware* (1975) and *Rumble-Tumble* (1977). These volumes give us the glimpses of the world by recording army life, espionage, hunting, mining, smuggling and political activity.

"A Little Sugar, a Little Tea," "Bombay Beware," "Maggie," "Bachcha Lieutenant," "Monal Hunt," and "Suliman's Courier" are some of his stories that deal with military life. In the words of G.S. Amur, these stories are "sentimental celebration of the army and its code, and are a comic celebration."[1]

Malgonkar's "Bachcha Lieutenant" is an interesting story that includes the incidents of Burma war. It is about loyalty and sacrifice which are expected of a solider. Jamadar Tukaram Shindey, "a jungle man, born and brought up in the jungles of North Kanara,"[2] would like to know the strategies of the Japanese army. So he preferred to go alone in the Burmese jungles. But Lt. Wilson, the young intelligence officer, who had not yet seen any "action" did not want to send him there alone. So he ordered him to go along with Ranga, another scout, to know the position of the enemy.

Shindey went into the jungle all alone. Ranga had been instructed by the Jamadar to pass on some message to the officer to the effect that he wanted to keep the enemy under observation.

Lt. Wilson grew restless because the scouts did not return from the jungle. He also wanted to find out how far the enemy's position was. He, along with two Jawans, advanced towards the enemy camp. Late in the afternoon, Jamadar Shindey was squirming behind a fallen tree where he identified Wilson's figure. While giving a warning to Wilson, he became a prey to the enemy's bullet and collapsed. Lt. Wilson ran madly towards Jamadar. He was relentless in his effort of saving the life of Jamadar. So he ran towards the cart track carrying the body on his shoulders. The enemies chased him continuously. The bullets riddled the two bodies making their limbs twitch with each hit.

Thus, the story reminds us of *Distant Drum* that deals with army life. Like Kiran Garud of *Distant Drum,* Lt. Wilson in this story lives upto the Regimental code of conduct. The ghastly death of the protagonist is vividly portrayed in the story.

"Bear on a Plate," "To Hold a Tiger," "Shikar Deluxe," and "Tiger Trouble" give an account of Malgonkar's preoccupation with hunting. His "Bear on a Plate" shows how a tiger shoot is managed. Mr. Elmer Finkelstein, a Texan, who has won sixteen crates of trophies goes to India for tiger shooting. He makes a request to Bagal Singh to guide him in hunting. In response to his request, Bagal Singh arranges for the hunting of a tiger in the Pilapani jungles. When Finkelstein succeeds in killing the "Demon-Leopard" of Pilapani. Bagal Singh applauds him thus:

> The oil-Sahib is today the envy of all the shikaris in India. A leopard with that kind of marking has not been shot since the days of Lord Hardinge. In all my shooting days I for one have never seen the like of him.[3]

Later Finkelstein wants to kill "bear," the most dangerous animal in the Indian jungle. Soon Bagal Singh makes arrangement for the hunting of the bear. Some hunters are asked to get themselves ready with a few rifles. The camera is ready to take pictures. Mr. Finkelstein is equally alert to kill the bear. All expect that the bear would come out of the bushes. But they are surprised to see the two grown up man-eaters and two half-grown cubs coming out of the bushes. They see "all charging towards them at a gallop."[4] They soon feel diffident and run away from there for protection.

The story ends dramatically where the bear looks intently into the lense of Mr. Finkelstein's German-made cine-camera. Thus, it delineates the failure of an ambitious hunter from Texas. In his stories that deal with military life and hunting activity, Malgonkar has shown that he "has a lively appreciation of Indian wild life . . . and has an intimate knowledge of military life."[5]

Malgonkar finds a way to articulate and organize his experience in an American business firm in Delhi. His "Fair Wind in Timber Land" concerns itself with a business deal between Bania Baburam, the business man, and Shamrao Maney, who lost all his wealth and "lived in a small village in the midst of heavy forest."[6] Baburam has prospered as a shop-keeper and had a virtual monopoly of the trade in 26 villages.

Shamrao needed about a thousand rupees for his daughter's marriage. Even all his 300 acres of jungle woodland might not fetch that amount for him. So he approached Baburam for money. The merchant gave him provisions to the tune of thirteen hundred and nineteen rupees. He was prepared to give him more only when he would surrender all his right on the jungle woodland. Shamrao agreed to the proposal and even signed on a paper to that effect. Baburam was happy because he had already earned a profit of more than 400 rupees on all the things he had sold to Shamrao.

Within a week, Baburam disposed the jungle land to the Kamalnath Industries Group of Bombay and got a net profit of about twelve thousand rupees. The story ends dramatically with the discovery of a new manganese site in the jungle land bought by Kamalnath Group of Industries. The land brings an unexpected piece of good fortune for Baburam on one hand and the Kamalnath Industries Group on the other. In the words of G.S. Amur, this story shows "a better insight into the psychology of the businessman and his practices."[7]

Malgonkar's "Thorn with a Thorn," "Hush" and "Cargo from Singapore" present the theme of smuggling. The title of "Thorn with a Thorn" is borrowed from a Marathi proverb, "you can extract a thorn with another thorn." The story begins with the Commissioner of Customs Department who narrates the racket of smuggling:

> Petty smuggling is annoying, but this sort of organized racket is far more serious. They only operate at night, of course, and whenever one of our launches gives chase, they make for the shallow water. Our launch cannot follow them there . . . those fishermen know it like the backs of their hands.[8]

These lines of the Commissioner give a vivid description of the act of smuggling. The Commissioner decides to curb this activity.

The scene of action is Chankoli in Goa where a lot of smuggling activity goes on. The Commissioner in the Department of Customs who is worried about this deputes Jayawant, his subordinate, to Chankoli. Jayawant who is conversant with the area, reaches Chankoli to fulfil his mission. Tantya Sabley, his boyhood friend, greets him there.

After a few days, Jayawat seeks Tantya's help in discovering the ring of smugglers operating through Chankoli. Surprisingly, Tantya stops his visits to Jayawant, his friend. But Jayawant, through his strong naval binoculars, would look at Tantya's "bronze figure hurling the mackerel net as no other fisherman in the harbour could."[9]

Having disappeared for a few days, Tantya goes to Jayawant one day. Immediately, the latter asks the former why he is not found in the company of the other fishermen. The former gives an evasive reply: "I fish where there is fish. . . . A good fisherman should never fish in fishless waters just because the others are there."[10]

Jayawant grows restless for he has not fulfilled his goal even after a three-month period. One day Jayawant receives information that a hundred bars of gold have been brought into Goa from Kuwait in an Arab dhow. Immediately, he, along with three constables and a hawaldar, goes to patrol the road by his jeep. Surprisingly, he sees the road blocked by the fallen trees. In utter disappointment, he gets back to Chamkoli the next day.

Jayawant notices Tantya's boat anchored in a backwater beyond the timber wharf. He knows well that no fisherman can even attempt to fish in that pool. He observes that Tantya waits there to retrieve something out of the water in darkness. Immediately, he and the two inspectors reach the spot and drag the boat to the bank. He collects from the boat four canvas bags full of gold bars. Thus, Jayawant succeeds in curbing the smuggling activity and also in extracting the thorn with another thorn.

"Pull-Push," "The Fixer," "Air-Conditioned," "A Pinch of Snuff" and "A Slice of the Melon" are a few of Malgonkar's stories that reveal his sensitiveness to political activity in India.

"Pull-Push" deals with the political affiliations of Indian servants. In the words of Amur, "this story is a metaphor for the pulls and pressures that the writer sees in operation at every level of our social and political life."[11] In this story Sukhpal, a class IV Government servant, succeeds in getting a transfer for his boss whom he does not like.

Malhotra, the boss, often shouts at Sukhpal, an insincere chaprasi in the Secretariat. But Sukhpal,

> a slumberer-in-corridors, a dawdler-between-errands, a misplacer-of-files, incurable tune-hummer and user of scented hair oil, he was also indolent, and immune to scoldings. No one wanted him as his office-boy but it is far easier to unseat a minister than to fire a member of what are called class IV Government servants.[12]

He tells his friends how he intends to send executives like Malhotra to remote places like Raihal.

Haveli Ram, a trade union leader, is the brother-in-law of Sukhpal. He has established contacts with ministers like Champaklal. Sukhpal approaches him and tells him that he wants to take revenge on Malhotra, the boss. He even requests his brother-in-law to put a word to the Minister and get a transfer for Malhotra to a remote place like Raihal. His brother-in-law concedes the demand.

The scene of action is shifted to the Secretariat. The boss is found again losing his temper on the indolent Sukhpal. He decides to send a letter to the Chief Secretary requesting him to transfer this insincere class IV employee to some other department. He writes the letter to that effect, puts it in a cover, seals it and asks the sergeant to hand it over to the Under Secretary personally.

Soon Sukhpal enters the room and hands over an envelope to his boss. The boss opens the cover and is disappointed to read it as it contains his own transfer orders. The boss who tries to get a transfer for the servant is himself transferred to a distant place.

This story deals with politics which reigns supreme in the day-to-day administration. In this world of politics, a class IV employee like Sukhpal, with his powerful political affiliations, can checkmate easily a top executive like Malhotra. The story does not over-step the bounds of dramatic suddenness.

It is pertinent to note the interrelationship of Malgonkar's novels and short stories from the point of view of their themes—army, hunting, trade, smuggling, politics and history. Though the themes are similar, one finds the difference between his novels and short stories with regard to the mood. If the characteristic mood of Malgonkar's mature novels is one of epic seriousness, the mood of his short stories, with a few exceptions, is essentially comic. This cleavage between his novels and short stories cannot be found in either Raja Rao's or Narayan's fiction.

Unlike his mature novels, the stories of Malgonkar are in a comic mood. Except for a few, the characters drawn from either aristocratic background or from upper strata of society, they engage our delighted attention rather than our profound concern. For example, in the stories that concern themselves with war and hunting, the characters who appear to be serious in the beginning turn out to be silly and jovial in the end. In "A Little Sugar, a Little Tea," Brigadier Murry inspects the company with utmost earnestness and finds that Major Maxwell, the officer-in-charge, is not there. Without taking any action against him, the Brigadier leaves for Delhi in a jovial mood. Even in "Maggie" Lieutenant Howard and General, the two army officers who are drawn towards Maggie, do not collapse when they come to know that their fiancee has married a Major in the U.S. army air-corps. Elmer Finkelstein in "Bear on a Plate" wants to kill "a man-devouring bear." But when four bears come out of the bush, the poor American runs away without attacking them.

Even in the stories that deal with trade and smuggling, we come across comic characters. For example, Shamnath, in "Blame the Army" entertains us with his success in solving the labour unrest in the Bluerock Company. Even in "Cargo from Singapore," the newspaper reporter entertains us with his plans. Similarly Lala Govind Sarup in "The Fixer," Nandalal Keshawaram in "Air-Conditioned" and Nanakaka in "A Pinch of Snuff" come to us as comic characters.

One finds the pattern of temporary disruption and then normalcy in most of the stories of Malgonkar. One can say, with utmost boldness, that his stories on War and hunting fall in this pattern. For example, in "Pack Drill" the soldiers who are anxious to attend the marriage of Subedar's daughter cannot do so because of the inspection. But soon they are allowed to attend the marriage. In "Suliman's Courier," Captain Mansingh is perturbed because he feels that the parcels consist of arms and ammunition. But soon he heaves a sigh of relief when he comes to know that they contain bottles of incense, cigars etc. The same pattern fits in in the rest of the stories.

Suspense and dramatic suddenness bind the stories of Malgonkar together. In his stories, as the plot progresses, it arouses expectations in the reader about the future course of events. The interplay of suspense and surprise is a prime source of strength of his plots. The effective surprise is one which turns out, in retrospect, to have been well grounded in what has gone before, even though we have hitherto made the wrong inference from the given facts of circumstances and character.

In almost all the short stories of Malgonkar, one finds the element of suspense which makes his stories grippingly interesting. Fox example, in "Pack Drill," one really wants to know whether the trainees are going to attend the marriage at Sonmala village or not. All of a sudden the writer reveals that they go to marriage without informing the Brigadier. In "Suliman's Courier" too, suspense regarding the contents of the packages is maintained throughout. All of a sudden, Holland opens the packages and finds cigars and perfume bottles in them. Similarly in "To Hold a Tiger," suspense regarding the protagonist's killing of the tiger is maintained. Only in the end it is dramatically said that the protagonist does not succeed in killing the animal. In "A Toast in Warm Wine," the exact scene of action is kept in suspense for a long time. The story ends dramatically with the protagonist receiving a cheque for Rs. 10,000/- Even in "Cargo from Singapore," one wants to know whether the protagonist is going to take revenge upon Mathrani, his enemy. "Air-Conditioned" sustains suspense with regard to the hiding of the bottles in the M.L.A's suitcase. Dramatically the M.L.A. tells the protagonist about the circumstances that have made him save the life of the protagonist.

Irony is one technique which Malgonkar employs in his short stories. Most of the titles are ironically used in the three volumes. Among the stories that deal with business and politics, one finds the amused observations made by the protagonist. "A Toast in Warm Wine" presents ironically the story of a former big-game hunter who tries hard to make a new career in manganese mining. Malgonkar's use of irony is revealed in his "Bondage." Godambi, the corrupt Deputy Collector, wants to take revenge against Ramsa Patil for exposing his corrupt practice. He humiliates Ramsa Patil at a public function and frees an orphan boy from "Bonded Labour." The writer passes on ironic remarks on the corrupt practices of the Deputy Collector. In "A Slice of the Melon," he passes ironic comments on the politicians who in the name of party funds, promote their material concerns.

NOTES

1. G.S. Amur, *Manohar Malgonkar* (New Delhi: Arnold Heinemann India, 1973), p. 27.
2. Manohar Malgonkar, *Bombay Beware*, p. 58.
3. Manohar Malgonkar, *A Toast in Warm Wine*, p. 153.
4. *Ibid.*, p. 154.
5. Haydn M. Williams, "Manohar Malgonkar: The Captains and The Kings," *The Journal of Indian Writing in English,* Vol. 8, Jan.-July 1980, p. 37.
6. Manohar Malgonkar, *Rumble-Tumble* (New Delhi: Orient Paperbacks, 1977), p. 101.
7. G.S. Amur, p. 34.
8. *A Toast in Warm Wine*, p. 101.
9. *Ibid.*, p. 104.
10. *Ibid.*, p. 105.
11. G.S. Amur, p. 36.
12. *A Toast in Warm Wine*, p. 117.

Rural Life Shaken to its Roots: Kamala Markandaya's *Nectar in a Sieve*

Rural life in the Indian literature in English could be found in its embryonic form in Lal Behari Day's *Govinda Samantha*, Behramji Malabari's *Gujarat and Gujaraties*, Coopoo Swamy's *Everyday Life in South India*, T. Ramakrishna Pillai's *Life in an Indian Village* and Nagesh Vishwanath Pai's *Stray Sketches in Chakmakpore*. The authors of these works have exploited ancient myths and folk-tales.

Towards the early twentieth century, writers began to stretch their imagination towards rural society, with a view to showing to the world the real India by writing mainly on rural themes. Some wrote with the first-hand observation of village life and others depicted it through the spectacles of books. In their vocation, they put forth the predilections of the villagers, their unflinching sensitiveness to nature, struggle for existence etc. set against the rural background. This naturally led to the emergence of rural novel in India.

To the tradition of rural novel in India belongs Venkataramani who in his *Murugan the Tiller* depicts primarily "the Gandhian ideal of going back to the village and secondly emphasizing the need for the traditional Indian way of living."[1] Raja Rao appears on the scene next. He in his *Kanthapura* offers a realistic account of the villagers and their ways. Next comes Mulk Raj Anand who in his *Coolie, Two Leaves and a Bud, The Village* and *Gauri* has fostered the tradition of rural novel in Indian writing in English.

After Independence, the Indian novel in English witnessed changes in regard to themes and techniques. The novelists freed themselves from voicing the political aspirations of their people in throwing away of the foreign rule. Most of them bestowed their attention on the teeming millions, particularly the problems of the villagers. As P.P. Mehta points out, "the rural poverty which was emphasized by the Government while presenting their first five year-plan has thrown up a new class of the novel."[2] Among the exponents of the new class of the novel are Bhabani Bhattacharya and Kamala Markandaya. These two novelists deal with the rural life comprehensively. Bhattacharya's *Music for Mohini* and Kamala Markandaya's *Nectar in a Sieve* are typical rural novels in the post-independence period.

Kamala Markandaya's *Nectar in a Sieve* presents a moving account of a tenant farmer Nathan and his family. It depicts the downfall of the peasant due to various factors like the vagaries of nature, the merciless zamindari system, and the industrialization represented by sinister tannery. Destroyed by industry and the curses of nature, the peasant and his family leave for the town, where their condition turns from bad to worse. He finds it difficult to cope with city life, and finally dies there leaving his beloved wife Rukmani. The poor Rukmani returns to her own village. The novel thus "is a tour de force on the peasant's life, their toil, their torture, their anguish, their suffering and above all their tragedy."[3]

The one element that draws some critical attention to this novel is a typical presentation of "rural life" with all its innocence and bliss. The scene of action is a village in southern India. The novelist presents a realistic account of rural India with all its sensitiveness to nature, convictions in traditions and attitudes to life. The subtitle "A Novel of Rural India" gives us a clue to the fact that it concerns itself with the typical rural life in India. The novelist delineates how the villagers become a prey to the vagaries of nature. Sometimes they face the loss of crops due to excessive rains and at other times the failure of rains. This calamity caused by nature is evident throughout the novel. Once the rains start pouring continuously, the village and its fields are drowned in water.

The trees are uprooted and the villagers are deprived of shelter. In Rukmani's words,

> After the fury of the night before, an unnatural stillness lay on the land. I went out to see if any thing could be saved of the vegetables, but the shoots and vines were battered and broken, torn from their supports and bruised; they did not show much sign of surviving. The corn field was lost. Our paddy field lay beneath a placid lake on which the children were already sailing bits of wood.
>
> Many of our neighbours fared much worse than we had. Several were homeless, and of a group of men who sheltered under a tree when the storm began six had been killed by lightning.[4]

This passage throws light on the effects of terrible cyclone that has spread the ripples of hysteria in the placid village.

The novelist gives an account of the utter failure of rains, the bane of seasons in India. Drought persists and the protagonist prays to gods for rain. The family is once again in the grip of severe drought which

> continued until we lost count of the time. Day after day the pitiless sun blazed down . . . great irregular fissures gaped in the land. Plants died and the grasses rotted, cattle and sheep crept to the river that was no more and perished there for lack of water, lizards and squirrels lay prone and gasping in the blistering sunlight. (77-78)

They lose the hope of tomorrow. Suddenly appears Shivaji, the agent of the landlord, and asks Nathan for lease money. The couple, in utter dismay, sell all their possessions like dhal, dried chillies and saries which could fetch them not even half the money they have to pay as rent to the land. This reflects the wretched condition of life that any Indian village faces every year.

The novel presents the sensitiveness of the protag(nature. In a way, it recounts the responses of the villa_ the beauty of nature. There is almost Keatsian sensuousness in some of the descriptions of the sights and sounds of the village and its surroundings. Rukmani, a newly-married woman, expresses her impressions of nature when she is on way to her husband's house:

> We rested, a half-hour before resuming our journey. The animals refreshed, began stepping jauntily again, tossing their heads and jangling the bells that hung from their red-painted horns. The air was full of the sound of the bells, and of birds, sparrows and bulbuls mainly, and sometimes the cry of an eagle, but when we passed a grove, green and leafy, I could hear minahs and parrots. It was warm, and, unused to so long a jolting, I fell asleep. (3)

Rukmani's early impressions of nature are typical of any villager in India. Rukmani's description of nature continues:

> Today, for instance, I could see the brook that ran near our paddy field so clearly that I felt I had but to stoop to feel its water wet on my hands. Yet that brook belongs to a part of my life that is finished . . . the water was clear but not swift running. . . . I tucked my sari up above my knees and stood in the river, scrubbing the clothes against a large flat stone. (5)

This is the experience of a dreamy-eyed romantic, lost in a world of beauty. Like Rukmani, most of the villagers in India are lost in the world of beauty.

A close study of the novel offers a detailed description of several customs and practices that obtain in India. The novelist's account of the christening ceremony of Rukmani's first son is evocative of rustic life. On the tenth day of the birth of the child, the whole village participates in the feast and rejoices in their good fortune. The Nathans prepare,

> mounds of rice tinting it with saffron and frying it in butter; made hot curries from chillies and dhal; mixed sweet; spicy dishes of jaggery and fruit; broiled fish; roasted nuts over the fire; filled ten gourds with coconut milk; and art plantain leaves on which to serve the food. (121)

The villagers also celebrate marriages in a grand manner. Ira's marriage is very vividly described by the novelist. On the wedding day of Ira, the whole village participates with utmost sincerity:

> The bridegroom arrived; his parents, his relatives, our friends, the priests. The drummer arrived and squatted outside awaiting permission to begin; the fiddler joined him. There should have been other magicians. . . . Now I brought out the stores I had put by month after month—rice and dhal and ghee, jars of oil, betel leaf, areca nuts, chewing tobacco and copra . . . as the light faded two youths appeared bearing a palanquin for the newly married couple, lowered it at the entrance to the hut for them to step into. (36-38)

The novelist's account of rural life is evocative of happy feelings.

Similarly the death ceremony is a distinct feature of the rustic people. The burial of Raja, the murdered son of Rukmani, is vividly described. Not only friends but relatives also attend the funeral:

> They pay their respects in silence, and when the sun rises the men pick the bier and depart; but the women stav behind, for this is the custom. (90)

The descriptions of the rituals can be read with gripping interest by any reader who would like to be conversant with the rural life.

Another important aspect that deals with the rural life is its pride in ancestral property. Rukmani, like a typical villager, takes pride in the hut built by her husband. She cries out when she is forced to leave her humble hut for town. Even Nathan thinks nostalgically about his own village:

> Better to starve where we were bred than live here . . . whatever happens, whatever awaits us, we must return. (167)

In the village, the crop is deemed dearer than the child. The villagers feel that the sowing of seed disciplines the body, the sprouting of the seed uplifts the spirit. Thus, the novel becomes "an epic of the Indian life at the grassroots, a full view of the village world where peasants grow and live . . . and their obstinate clinging to the soil, like the stumps withered all over but its roots delved in the earth."[4]

The novelist also presents the theme of technological invasion on the rural India. With the advent of tannery, the placid life of Rukmani is disturbed. It is primarily responsible for the decay of natural beauty in the rural area. With its occupation of the playground, it comes in the way of the life of the children also. It pollutes the whole atmosphere of the village.

The villagers become practically "hands" in the factory, thereby making life mechanical. Arjun and Thambi join the tannery against the will of their mother and create stir there and are sacked by the townsmen. They leave for Ceylon to work in a tea plantation there and never return. Ira sells herself to the townsmen in order to save her little brother Kuti. Raja, the fourth son of Rukmani, is beaten to death by a watchman of the tannery for an alleged theft of a costly hide. Murugan the third son of Nathan migrates to town with a view to seeking out his livelihood. Even Rukmani and her husband are forced to leave for the town to meet their son Murugan, because they have been evicted from the rented land, which has been purchased by the tannery owners. The labour crisis leads to the disruption of the harmony in the village. Consequently, Rukmani and her husband decide to go to town.

The novelist presents vividly the evil effects of zamindari system in the village. Nathan, a tenant farmer, must pay rent on the one hand, and support his family on the other. This has been going on for the past thirty years. But the tannery owners tempt the landlord and buy the land from him thereby causing dislocation of and disintegration in the family of Nathan. Though it is a land taken on lease, Nathan considers it to be his own. He constructs a hut and cultivates the land with utmost affection. As a tenant, Nathan is forced to pay the rent irrespective of the odds of nature. Hence "there was no money left—every pie had gone to pay the land dues. Nothing left to sell." (79) Nathan talks about the exploitation of the tenant farmers by the affluent landlord:

> Now the landlord can wring from us his money and care not for the misery he evokes, for indeed it would be difficult for any man to see another starve and his wife and children as well; or to enjoy the profits born of such travail. (73)

These lines reveal the misery faced by a small farmer in India.

A charge levelled against Kamala Markandaya is the use of language in her novels. Shyamala Venkateswaran comments: "*Nectar in a Sieve* fails not so much because of the factual inaccuracies but because the style totally fails to capture the sensibility of a village woman."[5] She seems to feel that a wife calling her husband by name is not a convention in the Indian society. But nowhere do we find Rukmani calling Nathan by name. It is only in sotto voce and that too only after her husband's death.

Markandaya in this novel has succeeded in using the language in keeping with the situations and characters. For example, one finds a clear distinction between the speech patterns of the townsmen, and those of the villagers. This is evident from the remark made by the villagers:

> They spoke in our language, but with an intonation which made it difficult for us to understand them. (26)

This only shows how the novelist is always conscious of using the language in keeping with situations and characters.

Nectar in a Sieve is the story of a village shaken to its roots by the onslaught of modern civilization. One is naturally reminded of Markandaya's other novel *The Coffer Dams* which deals with the theme of the technological invasion. Like any other Indian village, the village in *The Coffer Dams* has been enjoying the slumber of peace for generations. So far it has seen only the vagaries of nature that have interfered with the lives of its inhabitants. But, for the first time, they encounter the intrusion of the industry. In *The Coffer Dams,* the grunting mechanical marvels take away the sense of belonging from the hearts of the tribes. The sirens on the dam site are "wailing Devils"[6] to the villagers who have not known so far the wonder-works of machines. Industrialization gives rise to a series of problems. The clash of the masters with the labourers becomes an endemic feature. The rural beauty has been scarred by the technological invasion. The heroine's fancy for village life draws her away from her husband Clinton. The novel ends with a note of optimism that the rural India of the future can withstand the onslaught of mechanization and industrialization. Similarly, in *Nectar in a Sieve,* the bane of the advent of the tannery is dealt with. It drives away Rukmani to town but she, like the protagonist in *The Coffer Dams,* goes back to the village.

To conclude, we may say that *Nectar in a Sieve* is set in an anonymous village in southern India. It presents a rural society with all its predilections, belief in ancient customs, and disruption of life caused by nature and industrialization. The novel acquires a universality of appeal in that "Nathan and Rukmani are true representatives of rural society with all its traditions, cultures, rites and rituals, which face extinction under the impact of modern ideas so clumsily embraced by the new generation."[7] In the words of Kai Nicholson, Markandaya concentrates "entirely on the lives of rural Indians."[8]

NOTES

1. G.P. Sarma, *Nationalism in Indo-Anglian Fiction* (New Delhi: Sterling, 1978), p. 194.
2. P.P. Mehta, *Indo-Anglian Fiction: An Assessment* (Bareilly: Prakash, 1968), p. 248.
3. Hari Mohan Prasad, ed., "The Quintessence of Kamala Markandaya's Art," *Response: Recent Revelations of Indian Fiction in English* (Bareilly: Prakash, 1983), p. 159.
4. Kamala Markandaya, *Nectar in a Sieve* (Bombay: Jaico, 1982), pp. 40-41.
5. Shyamala Venkateswaran, "The Language of Kamala Markandaya's Novels," *The Literary Criterion*, Vol. IX (Winter 1970), p. 62.
6. Kamala Markandaya, *The Coffer Dams* (Delhi: Hind Pocket Books, 1969), p. 137.
7. Ramesh K. Srivastava, "Markandaya's *Nectar in a Sieve* as a Tragedy" *The Indian Journal of English Studies*, Vol. 23 (1983), p. 109.
8. Kai Nicholson, *Presentation of Social Problems in the Indo-Anglian and the Anglo-Indian Novel* (Bombay: Jaico, 1972), p. 117.

A Political Novel on India: Salman Rushdie's *Midnight's Children*

Salman Rushdie's magnum opus, *Midnight's Children*, is a novel on india that deals with Indian independence, partition and social problems. It is a political novel remarkably covering three generations of Adam Aziz, Saleem Sinai and Adam Sinai from 1910 to 1977.

Midnight's Children runs into three parts. Part I concerns itself with the events that took place in India from 1915 to 1947. Part II deals with the childhood of Ahmed Sinai, the protagonist. Part III is primarily on emergency operations and brutalities in India during the seventies. Surprisingly, the fortunes of the protagonist are similar to those of the post-Independence India. Rushdie weaves contemporary events—political and historical—into the main spectrum of the novel to produce the singleness of effect. As the narrator in the novel observes:

> I must work fast, faster than Scheherazade, if I am to end up meaning—yes, meaning—something. I admit it: above all things, I fear absurdity. (4)

These lines of the protagonist throw light on Rushdie's view of a novel.

> Saleem the protagonist, was born in the city of Bombay. . . . Once upon a time . . . on August 15th, 1947. And the time? The time matters, too, Well then . . . at the precise instant of India's arrival at independence. (3)

Saleem narrates the story of his grandfather, Adam Aziz, a young doctor who returned from Germany with a good medical degree. Adam was in search of his moorings like other Muslims of the times. One fine morning, he was taken to the house of Ghani Sahib, an affluent landlord, in Kashmir. He was asked to examine Naseema, the ailing daughter of the landlord. He bent his body and examined the patient thoroughly. Ironically, he married her later with "A-I fine dowry."

Soon Adam gets the job of a doctor at Agra University. While he is shifting his family to Agra, he witnesses the Jallianwala Bagh Massacre in Amritsar. The authorial voice runs thus: "I confess . . . I have noticed a thin crack, like a hair, appearing in my wrist, beneath the skin. . . . No matter. We all owe death a life." (36) The narrative account here is in the shape of a selective recalling of the past from the vantage point of the present.

In Agra, Adam Aziz witnessed many events like the formation of "Free Islam Convocation" and the emergence of Muslim league. One fine morning Nadir Khan, the Secretary of Mian Abdullah, fled from his assassins and took refuge in the basement of Adam Aziz's house. He soon courted Mumtaz, the eldest daughter of Aziz. Meanwhile, Major Zulfikar was engaged in capturing Nadir Khan. But the Khan managed to skip him. Ahmed Sinai, a top-ranking businessman in Delhi, went to marry Mumtaz who became Amina for Ahmed.

After the communal riots in Delhi, Ahmed decided to invest his resources in "real estates" in Bombay where Saleem was born on the midnight stroke of August 15th, 1947 at the time when India became independent. Saleem Sinai, the midnight child, bagged the most covetous prize from *The Times of India* besides a letter of "intense" appreciation from the then Prime Minister, Jawaharlal Nehru. Ahmed and Amina lost their real child by the baby swop done by the nurse Mary Pereira.

Part two of the novel begins with the financial crisis faced by the family of Ahmed Sinai. After a few trials and tribulations, the members of Ahmed Sinai's family migrate to Pakistan with a view to settling in Karachi permanently. They become victims of 1965-war.

Part three of the book, which runs like a fantasy, dwells upon politics directly, exaggerating the Emergency operations. Saleem grows along with India with all her excesses of emergency, her inner turbulence and the political suppression. Thus, Rushdie's *Midnight's Children* exhibits ironically the contemporary events that took place in India.

In this novel, the novelist ingeniously weaves the personal story of Saleem and his growth into the story of India and her development. Owing to the forces of circumstances, the parents of Saleem leave for Karachi with a view to settling down there permanently. Soon Saleem records the important events that led to the escalation in the relations between India and Pakistan:

> Entirely without my help, India conquered Goa. . . . I played no part in the acquisition of large-scale US aid for Pakistan, nor was I to blame for Sino-Indian border skirmishes in the Aksai-Chin region of Ladakh: the Indian census of 1961 revealed a literacy level of 23.7 percent . . . and in the elections of 1962, the All-India Congress won 361 out of 494 seats in the Lok Sabha, and over 61 percent of all State Assembly seats. (351)

Besides the deterioration of relations between India and Pakistan one notices excesses of the emergency operation. In a way the disintegration of the midnight's children's conference goes together with the lack of the spirit of nationalism in India. The toils and moils confronted by the members of family of Saleem are similar to those of the brutalities and traumas faced by the post-independence Indian psyche. In the words of William Walsh, "astonishing staple is composed of element of magic and fantasy, the grimmest realism."[2]

The narrative technique is one aspect that can draw considerable critical attention. One notices a continuous oscillation between the fictitious and the factual. In the very opening paragraph of the novel, the narrator makes a statement about his mode of narration:

> And there are so many stories to tell, too many, such an excess of intertwined live events miracles places rumors, so dense a commingling of the improbable and the mundane! I have been a swallower of lives; and to know me, just the one of me, you'll have to swallow the lot as well. (5)

From this passage, one observes the interest of the narrator in intertwining the improbable and the mundane, thereby preparing us for the extremely fanciful and the extremely factitious. In fact, the novelist fuses these two extremes and "opposing ends of the fictional spectrum into another kind of symbiosis."[3] One also notices the novelist freeing himself from the rigour of the plot of a well-made novel. The narrator is very particular that history should add upto something and give some meaning to his novel.

The narrative in the novel is in the shape of a selective recalling of the past from the vantage point of the present. The reader finds innumerable episodes of the past that are tied together by the person of the narrator. These episodes go together with the chronology of the development of the narrator. This technique rightly accommodates the chronological progression of the socio-cultural and the politico-cultural scene of the country.

The personal account is clothed in heavy trappings of fantasy and the public part is properly seasoned to produce, what Saleem calls, "the chutnification of history." To the social and political details are added various mixtures of spicy stuff—anecdotes, mythological lore, diverting comedy—all with the effective use of language.

The novel is not just a record of the contemporary historical and political events; it is an artistic recreation of these events. Naturally one observes the novelist dealing with not merely the story of Saleem but particularly a human story. Thus, transcending the confines of the particular, the novel acquires universality of appeal.

There is something remarkable in the experiments with language to capture the milieu of the contemporary events of the day in this political novel, *Midnight's Children.* In the words of M.L. Raina, "No Indian novelist has had the courage to handle English language with gaiety and joyousness of Rushdie."[4] Rushdie's mastery of language is total and more effective than most of the Indian novelists in English. In his own words, "English, no longer an English language, grows from many roots, and those whom it once colonized are carving out large territories within the language for themselves."[5]

To make his language more effective, Rushdie employs certain linguistic devices which make the novel more appealing and powerful. It is pertinent to dwell upon the element of rhetoric in the novel. Rushdie's account of the city-riot of Amritsar is quite graphic:

> Amritsar dung was fresh and (worse) redundant. Nor was it all bovine. It issued from the rumps of the horses between the shafts of the city's many tongas, ikkas and gharries, and mules and men and dogs attended nature's calls, mingling in a brotherhood of shit. (31)

This juxtaposition of mules, men and dogs into one brotherhood of shit is suggestive of the author's disgust with the city.[6]

Similar descriptions are found with regard to the city of Karachi. Through such juxtapositions, Rushdie ventilates his disgust with the cities in India as well as those in Pakistan.

Rushdie is dexterous in employing the technique of irony in the description of the post-independence India:

> I remain, today, half-convinced than in that time of accelerated events and diseased hours the past of India rose up to confound her present; the new-born, secular state

> was being given an awesome reminder of its fabulous antiquity, in which democracy and votes for women were irrelevant . . . so that people were seized by atavistic longings, and forgetting the new myth of freedom reverted to their old ways, their old regionalist loyalties and prejudices, and the body politic began to crack. (294)

The passage ironically comments on the "angst-ridden mind" of the novelist. The novelist's account of the declaration of emergency is again a record of the awful situation prevailing in India. Ironically, the growth of Saleem Sinai is akin to the post-independence psyche. The novelist subtly fuses the birth of Parvati's bastard child with the bastardly excesses of the emergency:

> Dark clouds were gathering in political skies as well: in Bihar, where corruption inflating hunger illiteracy landlessness ruled the roost, Jaya Prakash Narayan led a coalition of students and workers against the governing Indian Congress, in Gujarat, there were riots . . . and what was being born while something grew in Parvati's belly? (491)

The passage is a brisk abstract of the brutalities and excesses that obtained during the emergency in India.

Rushdie's *Midnight's Children* is a sort of comic epic genre, a form which is a fusion of Homeric, mythic and tragic connotations. This novel spreads through six decades and almost three generations of India's pre- and post-independence history. It is an epic in the sense that "it tries to describe" or contain "an India whose stories are too innumerable to be "contained."[7] Throughout the book, one finds the novelist stepping towards "that involvement with mighty events and public lives from which I would never again be free . . . never, until the widow." (205)

Surprisingly, in this novel, ends are contained in beginning, beginnings in ends. As each end is the beginning of a new story, the narrative is circular and never-ending. Moreover, this is an epic that cannot contain all the untold stories that are waiting to be told. One finds the epic form becoming a strategy of liberation and the comic becoming too painful to be expressed. There is the tragedy of Adam Aziz depicted in comic, mythic and surreal terms.

The tragedy of Adam is his identity crisis. Having received training as a physician in Germany for five years, he comes back to the Kashmir valley and follows the traditional customs. As he offers prayer of his ancestral religion, he becomes reminiscent of Heidelberg days. He learns, along with medicine and politics, that India like radium has been discovered by the Europeans. He recalls his friends mocking his prayer with their anti-ideologies.

The description of Adam Aziz runs in the comic epic tradition: "Forward he bent, and the earth, prayermat-covered, curved up towards him. And now it was the tussock's time . . . it smote him upon the point of the nose." (6) This tragic situation is expressed in mythic and surreal terms:

> Three drops fell. There were rubies ana diamonds. And my grandfather, lurching upright, made a resolve. And was knocked forever into that middle place, unable to worship a God in whose existence he could not wholly disbelieve. Permanent alteration: a whole. (6)

This is a pain of someone cut off from an authentic indigenous past, a past that he senses exists only as a property of its colonial masters. A whole identity is replaced by a literal hole which is later transformed into a perforated sheet by peeping through which Adam Aziz falls in love with Naseema. But the hole is so insidious that it devours everyone it touches. So Naseem can only internalize the hole and become an agonized person like her husband. No wholesome relationships can emerge.

Saleem's character is very ably delineated in this novel.

Saleem serves as a choric commentator, because he narrates the events of the past, describes the present episodes, and does not hesitate to make oracular statements with regards to future. He promises a story but puts forth his confusions which transcend the confines of the particular. He weaves contemporary historical scenes into his narration with a view to making it more authentic. He does not hesitate to choose the extremely fanciful and thoroughly realistic situations. In the narration, one may not find any well-made plot, but one finds a unity of action because the narrator works fast in passing on his meaning. His midnight birth is linked with the future history of India.

Saleem's birth, babyhood, boyhood and adulthood are associated with the phases of the Indian political arena. He is born grotesque who goes on adding to his deformities as he develops, and is constantly changing. In his own words, he has embarked upon an "heroic programme of self-enlargement . . . armies of handkerchiefs, regiments of nappies found their way into the large washing-chest in mother's bathroom . . . shedding rubbish from various apertures." (145) This is symbolic of the muddled and chaotic condition that obtained during the emergence of independence.

Though Saleem narrates the story and participates in the events he becomes for some days invisible while being transported from Bangladesh to India. Touching India, he becomes visible. In a way he is "angst-ridden youngman" representing everyone in the world. He is alienated and gives vent to his anger. He says of himself:

> Who what am I? My answer! I am the sum total of everything that went before me, of all I have been seen done, of everything done—to—me. I am everyone everything whose being-in-the world affected was affected by mine. . . . I repeat for the last time: to understand me, you'll have to swallow a world." (457-58)

This passage throws light on the fact that Saleem is "one and the many a man and monster participant and voice—all rolled into one."[8]

Thus, Rushdie's *Midnight's Children* is an ironic commentary on the major political events that took place between 1947 and 1978. Like a historian, Rushdie records major historical events and like an artist he recreates history. The narrative and the theme go together presenting the personal as well as the untold story of the Indian subcontinent. It has to be admitted that *Midnight's Children* gives a fairly authentic history of contemporary India in the matter of facts."[9]

NOTES

1. Salman Rushdie, *Midnight's Children* (New York: Avon Books), 1982.
2. William Walsh, *India and the Novel, the Present*, ed. Boris Ford (Middlesex: Penguin Books, 1983), p. 257.
3. T.N. Dhar, "Micro Macro Symbiosis: the Form of Salman Rushdie's *Midnight's Children*," *The Journal of Indian Writing in English*, Vol. 13, January 1985, p. 17.
4. M.L. Raina, "History as Pantomime," *New Quest*, May-June (1982), p. 172.
5. Salman Rushdie, "The Empire Writes Back With a Vengeance," *The Times*, July 3, 1982.
6. T.N. Dhar, p. 21.
7. Falizia Afzal-Khan, "Myth De-Bunked: Genre and Ideology in Rushdie's *Midnight's Children* and *Shame*," *Journal of Indian Writing in English*, Vol. 14, No.1, Jan. 1986, p. 52.
8. T.N. Dhar, p. 20.
9. Uma Parameswaran "Autobiography as History," *The Toronto South Asian Review*, Summer 1982, Vol. 1, No. 2, p. 60.

Shame: A Point of View

Rushdie's third novel *Shame,*[1] in a way, is a companion piece to *Midnight's Children.* "It seems to me," Rushdie remarks, "that everything in both books has had to do with politics and with the relationship of the individuals and history."[2] Rushdie who has "dazzled the world with his extraordinary vision in *Midnight's Children* now surpasses even that triumph" in *Shame.*[3] While his *Midnight's Children* is a stupendous evocation of the evolution of India since Independence, *Shame* is about what happened to the other half of the subcontinent after 1947."[4] The novelist "expatiates upon the sins of Pakistan on the basis of his spiritual bond with that country."[5] The novel rests on the two poles of shame and shamelessness.

Shame depicts the fate and fortunes of two families—Raza Hyder and Iskander Harappa. Omar Khyyam Shakil is born as the common son of Munnee, Bunny and Chhunni, the three sisters who shared automatic and simultaneous symptoms of pregnancy. He gets out to marry the deformed Sufiya Zinobia, the daughter of Raza Hyder, the army officer, who, after a coup becomes the President of the country. Iskander Harappa, the dethroned President, is hanged. All political parties are banned, judiciary is subverted and elections are cancelled. One notices the grip of Martial Law Administration after the paralysis of democracy. The story closes with the revenge taken by the three mothers with the help of Omar Khayyam.

Shame expatiates extensively on the theme of shame and also encompasses various nuances that are associated with it. It runs on three levels—the political, the cultural and the social. On the political level, the novel runs like a document on the contemporary political situation in Pakistan. It may appear that the novelist concerns himself with the story of Raza Hyder and Iskander Harappa, the two powerful political leaders of the country. One may be tempted to draw parallels in the story of General Zia and Zulfikar Bhutto. The novelist explores in depth the Iskander-Raza Plot, "a very macho book—all about careerism, cops, politics, revenge, assassinations, excursions, blood and guts." He even presents various strategies employed by these two families—Raza Hyder and Iskander Harappa. He comes out overtly how shame is the result of excessive humiliation and that it certainly leads to violence. Naturally politicians who take recourse to the methods of repression are bound to fall one day or the other.

On the cultural level, the novelist draws our attention to poets and artists who are punished in Pakistan. A reputed poet in Karachi is put in jail for his patriotic compositions. Besides being tortured in an inhuman fashion, he "had been hung upside-down by the ankles and beaten, as if he were a new-born baby whose lungs had to be coerced into action so that he could squeal." (28) The plight of the poet reflects ostensibly the state of affairs prevailing in Pakistan.

There is the theme of the social mores of the backward and superstitious Islamic society that multiplies on shame through limitless repression breeding violence. In fact, this leads to psychological horrors in society. In the words of the narrator,

> Repression is a seamless garment; a society which is authoritarian in its social and sexual codes, which crushes its women beneath the intolerable burdens of honour and propriety, breeds repressions of other kinds as well. Contrariwise: dictators are always—or at least in public, on other people's behalf—puritanical. (173)

Thus, the theme of shame, "as depicted through the book takes on a zig-zag trajectory, with interesting results."[7]

Rushdie's art of characterization of this novel has drawn considerable critical attention. Omar Khayyam represents the comic vituperation of the murky political history of Pakistan. He is born of three recluse-spinsters who keep secret which of their wombs bore him on his grandfather's deathbed.

He often wants an escape from the oppressive protection of his three virgin mothers in Nishapur. He discovers that the personal shame is only a microcosmic form of the national shame he sees abroad. His ruminations at the end of the novel throw light on his desperate situation:

> I can confess to many things. Fleeing-from-roots, obesity, drunkenness, hypnosis. Getting girls in the family way, not sleeping with my wife, too-many-pine-kernels, peeping-tommery as a boy. . . . I confess to social climbing, to only-doing-my-job, to being cornerman in other people's wrestling matches. I confess to fearing sleep. (33)

Sufiya Zinobia is another character in the novel with considerable qualities of shame. Rushdie "personifies in her the shame of Pakistan." The novelist had the first hand knowledge of a Paksitani girl who is murdered by her father in the East end of London for allegedly having made love to a white boy and brought "such a dishonour upon her family that only her blood could wash away the stain." (123)

Sufiya Zinobia seems to have grown out of the corpse of the murdered girl in England. Caught between two cultures, she becomes a sacrificial scapegoat in expiation of the guilt her parents feel for having transplanted themselves in an alien land.

Through the disfigurement of Sufiya, Rushdie creates an oppressive world that becomes really grotesque. The reader no longer recognizes her as a character, as "she evolves into a myth and a legend, a beast, lusty for kill stalking the country, naked, matted with grime and blood."[9]

Rushdie dwells upon the triggers of violence within

Sufiya. The first outburst is a demoniac wringing of necks of Pinkie Aurangzeb's two hundred and eighteen turkeys. The second outburst is an attempted wringing of the neck of Naveed's husband, Talvar. There are subsequent instances of violence. The novelist seems to think that, if Sufiya, who is shame, is alienated in Pakistan, what remains then is unalienated shamelessness:

> What's the opposite of *Shame?* What's left when "sharam" is subtracted? That's obvious; shamelessness. (39)

Through the story of Omar Khayyam and Sufiya Zinobia, the novelist has presented an axis which lies between shame and shamelessness.

The greatness of the novel lies in the recreation of contemporary Indian history. The novel contains vivid presentation of history in the plot involving the relationships between the two important architects of Pakistan's history—Raza Hyder and Iskander Harappa. In the words of R.S. Pathak: "The novel tries to highlight complex networks of transcultural relationships between the individual and historical forces."[10] The treatment of events as well as characters is artistic in terms of history. For example, the novelist talks about various historical situations that obtain in Pakistan:

> History was old and rusted, it was a machine nobody had plugged in for thousands of years, and here all of a sudden it was being asked for maximum output. Nobody was surprised that there were accidents. . . . No, it's more than that: there are things that cannot be permitted to be true. (82)

Rushdie runs wildly about like a time traveller who has lost his magic capsule and fears he will never emerge from the disintegrating history of his race.

Some of the characters in the novel seem to negate history. Omar Khayyam descended upon the cohorts of history like a wolf on the fold. To Raza Hyder, the recalling of history is merely a "rite of blood." Bilquis is suspicious of history and pushes the past away like a poor relation.

The uniqueness about Rushdie's treatment of history also lies in his idea of illusionary fictional reality. For example, the locale of *Shame* is

> not Pakistan, or not quite. There are two countries, real and fictional. . . . My story, my fictional country exist like myself, at a slight angle to reality. I have found this off-centring to be necessary; but its value is, of course, open to debate. My view is that I am not writing only about Pakistan. (29)

We know that on the surface level the country is Pakistan, but on the deeper level, it may be any country where forces of repression operate. It is here that the novel transcends the confines of the particular. As the novelist says:

> I build imaginary countries and try to impose them on the ones that exist. I, too, face the problem of history: what to retain, what to dump, how to hold on to what memory insists on relinquishing, how to deal with change. And to come back to the "roots" idea, I should say that I haven't managed to shake myself free of it completely. (87-88)

This shows how the novelist sorts out events judiciously and gives imaginative colourings to his plot. As Timothy Brennan rightly observes, "As though fearing reprisals, *Shame* hides history in allusive references to the past which are buried in casual place names and family titles, and ironic reincarnations of figures from legend."[11]

There are layers of irony in the novel. There is the use of the situational and verbal irony here. The description of the 40th day celebration of the death of old Shakil, father of the three sisters, is ironically done. The dumb waiter, ironically, is not a man but an instrument of communication of the three scandalized sisters to communicate with the outside world at the time of their confinement. Another instance of irony is that Moulana Dawood is decorated in his own town with the Necklace of Shoes. The details regarding Raza Hyder's family are also given ironically. Ironically, God does not find a place for himself in Pakistan which is thought to be a holy country of God. To give a few instances of verbal irony, Omar Khayyam is named after a poet with an expectation of courting the Muse but ironically no quatrains issue forth from his pen. Pakistan indicates a holy place but in the novel it turns out to be a center of brutality and grotesqueness. Sufiya Zinobia is a beauty as well as a beast. As the novelist rightly explains, to comprehend her is to acknowledge savagery as a constituent element in national make-up, recognition of which shatters a nation's concept of itself.

Rushdie also employs the technique of parallels and contrasts. We may include in the list of parallels the following: just as evil days have fallen on Pakistan, the families of the main characters in the novel are doomed to unforeseen circumstances. Just as one notices the confrontation between the two families—Raza Hyder and Iskander Harappa—one observes similar confrontation between the forces of shame and shamelessness. The deformity of Sufiya Zinobia is contrasted with the charming nature of Good News. There is also a contrast in temperaments between Omar Khayyam and Babar.

Just as *Midnight's Children* concerns itself with the political scene that obtained in India, *Shame* delineates the events that have happened since independence in Pakistan. While recording the events, the novelist likes to underline his message also. He aims at showing how shame is a part of the architecture of the society in a country like Pakistan where

> Shameful things are done; lies, loose living, disrespect for one's elders, failure to love one's national flag, incorrect voting at elections, over-eating, extramarital sex

> . . . smuggling, throwing one's wicket away at the crucial point of a Test Match; and they are done shamelessly. (122)

Through the story of Sufiya and Omar Khayyam, the novelist throws light on the absurdities that obtain in the world of repression. In *Shame*, Sufiya Zinobia "seems to blush for everyone in the novel and is understood as being what the novel is about. She is a human animal decapitating and killing everything from turkeys and babies to her husband."[12] Through the fusion of fact and fiction, Rushdie mesmerizes the readers. The two political figures acquire universality of appeal because of their careful employment of various strategies in the realm of politics.

It is perhaps for the use of language that Rushdie's *Shame* has earned itself a place in the literary halls of fame, One finds in the novel nasty and crude expressions of cynical frankness. For example, Old Shakil calls his three daughters "whores" and condemns his city as "a hell hole." Hasmat Bibi curses the owner of a mule thus: "May your grand sons urinate upon your pauper's grave." Isky Harappa abuses Raza Hyder by calling him "a seducer of his grandmother's pet mongrel bitch." The employment of scandalous and foul language "has both structural and thematic significance."[13]

The novel bristles with felicitous phrases. The chapters themselves are fraught with such felicities of expression. For example, Bilquis has an unforgettably powerful nickname of Khansi-ki-rani or Queen of Coughs. The place where the three sisters look forward to transact their amorous affairs is called the "Dumb-waiter." The description of the doctor and instruments of medical students is fraught with felicitous expression:

> What's a doctor, after all?—A legitimized voyeur, a stranger whom we permit to poke fingers and even hands into places we would not permit most people to insert so much as a finger tip, who gazes on what we take most

> trouble to hide; a sister-at-bedsides, an outsider admitted to our most intimate moments, birthdeath etc, anonymous, a minor character, yet also paradoxically, central, especially at the crisis. (49)

This passage shows that Rushdie has succeeded eminently in the use of felicitous expressions in his language.

Rushdie does not hesitate to use a few Urdu expressions with a view to adding Indian sensibility to his novel. For example, the pawnbroker is called "a wide eyed chalacksahib." Naveed Hyder comments on marriage thus: "Marriage . . is freedom. You stop being someone's daughter and become someone's mother instead, ek dum, fut-a-fut, pronto." (155) Raza Hyder and his people wept with pride. He "has taken the Aansu-ki-wadi." (79) These expressions add the Indian flavour to the language and intensify the meaning of the novel.

The novel abounds in quotations and references to a variety of literary sources. Rushdie's aim is not to collect quotations and make references but to raise echoes. What interests him is the penumbra of universal sentiment around the particular expressions used by these famous authors. He almost weaves these into the central motif of shame. "The Dumb waiter" that echoes the absurdity of a Harold Pinter play documents the unexpressed fears and tensions of the three sisters. The references to "a Hanged Man" remind us of Frazer's *The Golden Bough* which offers a comparative study of the beliefs and institutions of mankind. "Affairs of Honour" suggests medieval knight errantry. "The woman in the veil" alludes both to the Bible and to the Hawthorne story about the veiled minister. "Judgment Day" is an allusion to the doomsday, a concept common to all religions. The title of the novel, with its connotation of the existential angst called shame, is reminiscent of Kafka's *The Trial*, a work cited within the text. (113) These references to various literary sources are intertwined into the central idea of shame, the emotion that begins in a sense of guilt and leads to violation of other people, violence to neighbours, and eventually to self-destruction and to more shame.

To conclude, one may say that Rushdie's *Shame* deals with the central motif of shame that runs through the psyche of several characters as a subterranean force and finally acts as a shuttle that pulls into shape several strands of the shameful story of "shame."

NOTES

1. Salman Rushdie, *Shame* (New Delhi: Rupa, 1983).
2. Gordon Wise, Interview with Salman Rushdie, *Gentleman*, Feb, 1984, p. 57.
3. Quoted on the blurb of the novel.
4. Sunil Sethi, "Rushdie's Revenge," a review of *Shame* in *India Today*, August 15, 1983, p. 122.
5. Sushila Singh, "*Shame:* Salman Rushdie's Judgement on Pakistan," *Studies in Indian Fiction in English*, ed. G.S. Balarama Gupta (Gulbarga: JIWE Publications, 1987), p. 14.
6. Dilip Fernandez, "Such Angst, Such Loneliness, Such Rootlessness," *Gentleman*, Feb. 1984, p. 100.
7. Thakur Guruprasad, "The Zig-Zag Trajectory of Shame in Rushdie's Novel," *Commonwealth Fiction,* ed. R.K. Dhawan (New Delhi: Classical, 1988), p. 51.
8. Sushila Singh, p.19.
9. Susan Oommen, "Fictional Intent in Rushdie's *Shame*," *The Literary Criterion*, Vol. 20, No. 2, p. 39.
10. R.S. Pathak, "History and Individual in the Novels of Rushdie," *Three Contemporary Novelists*, ed. R.K. Dhawan (New Delhi: Classical, 1985), p. 215.
11. Timothy Brennan, "*Shame*'s Holy Book," *The Journal of Indian Writing in English*, Vol. 16, No. 2 (July 1988), p. 211.
12. Adil Jussawalla, "Rushdie's *Shame*, Problems in Communication," *Studies in Indian Fiction in English*, p. 7.
13. D.S. Mishra, "Narrative Techniques of Salman Rushdie's *Shame*," *Punjab University Research Bulletin* (Arts), 1987, p. 40.

A Conversation with Raja Rao

PBR: Do you feel that your background of the ancient Brahmin descent has had any influence in making you a writer?

RR: I think it did a little.

PBR: You seemed to have learned philosophy in Urdu and some Islamic theology in Salar Jung's Madarsa-e-Aliya in Hyderabad. Do you think that this philosophical background has ever shaped you as a creative artist?

RR: I learned Sufism there. This appears in my short stories.

PBR: It was said that you were interested in the river Ganga and that you were busy in writing a book on her. Have you ever published any book dealing with the Ganga?

RR: Just ten days ago, it was published in India. Someone sent me a copy of it. The title is "The Ganges Remembered."

PBR: In an interview published in *The Illustrated Weekly of India* (January 5, 1964), you came out with your view of literature thus: "Literature as 'Sadhana' is the best life for a writer. . . . All this may sound terribly Indian, but it is not so really. Valery, Rilke and Kafka, for instance, are as close to this view as Tagore in looking upon literature as Sadhana." Will you please elaborate on the Western writers's dedication to the spiritual discipline?

RR: Kafka deeply felt literary creation as Sadhana. Similarly, Rilke looks upon literature as Sadhana.

PBR: E.M. Forster, like you, aligned himself with the city of Hyderabad. Did you ever meet him there? If so, what impressions have you formed on Forster as a writer?

RR: It was I who was instrumental in asking Natwar Singh to edit a book on E.M. Forster. I even contributed an article to it.

PBR: In your earliest writings in Kannada, you eulogize your motherland thus: "O Mother India! at your feet I have been blessed with a glimpse of the supreme spirit. I may leave you and go to your sisters, but I can never forget you." Having lived in the USA for long, do you still hold the same view of owing your inheritance to India?

RR: Yes I do. I tell my American friends that America has only a four hundred year history, Europe has about a 1500 to 2000 year history, but India has four thousand years of splendid heritage. I also tell them that Greece and Rome are the suburbs of India.

PBR: This pertains to the epigraph to your *The Cow of the Barricades and Other Stories.*

On all the roads I go, they suffer
The hermit and the householder
When I tell them the truth, they are angry
And I cannot lie.

How far is this realized in your first collection of short stories?

RR: They mostly deal with the sufferings of human beings. So the epigraph.

PBR: In the Foreword to your novel *Kanthapura*, you said, "Our method of expression has to be dialect which will someday prove to be as distinctive and colourful as the Irish or the American. Time alone will justify it." Do you feel that Indian English has acquired distinction and colour as American English?

RR: Yes, I certainly feel that Indian English has acquired

such distinction. When I read some of the journals from India, I feel that they have overcome their Victorian English. They write very good English.

PBR: The epigraph to *The Serpent and the Rope*—waves are nothing but water. So is the sea—is from the sayings of Atmananda. But I find this to be more parallel to Sankara's Hymn on clouds and water. What is your comment on this?

RR: You are absolutely correct. My guru is an advaita. Naturally, he explains the advaita philosophy of Sankara.

PBR: In *The Serpent and the Rope*, Rama declares, "Bombay is a barbaric city . . . it had no right to exist." Do you think that Aryan wisdom, symbolizing beauty, wisdom and purity, is not preserved there in the city of Bombay?

RR: It is really dirty. It is more westernized.

PBR: Between Indian philosophical and religious thought and the Western philosophical position—which has influenced you more in the writing of your latest novel, *The Chessmaster* ?

RR: I always follow the Indian tradition, but I cannot understand where exactly I have been influenced by the Western philosophical position. *The Chessmaster and His Moves* expounds the cosmic tapestry of India. India contributed "zero" to the world. I took a cue from Ramanujan's concept of Mathematics and proceeded. There is no question of western influence on me.

PBR: Have you any particular message to convey in *The Chessmaster and His Moves* ?

RR: You read it and react to it.

PBR: Did you suffer from critics's lack of experience of the impersonal and the Absolute? If so, will you please specify?

RR: Many a time, especially, with regard to my *Chessmaster*, critics have not understood the seven or eight levels of meaning of the text. So, most of them have written bad reviews of the book. Similarly, they have searched in my work for the East-West dialogue which is not there at all.

PBR: In your fiction, I find your protagonists are always modelled on you. Do you agree?

RR: No. The imagination of mine found a concrete shape in the protagonists in my work.

PBR: You seemed to have conducted research on the influence of India on Irish literature under the guidance of Prof. Cazamian at the university of Paris. Can you possibly explain the Indian factors that have influenced Irish literature?

RR: Yes. I find similarities between India and Ireland. Mysticism is one such element. W.B. Yeats translated some Upanishads into English. Tagore had some influence on Ireland.

PBR: What comments can you offer on present Indian writing in English in general and of Indian fiction in particular?

RR: I am not a critic at all.

PBR: What is your answer to the critics who say that your novels sometimes overdo the scenes relating to love and sex?

RR: They are not correct. What is Sivalinga in a temple? It is the Yoni of Parvati and the linga of Siva. In temples, we find a similar picture. Read Kalidasa's *Abhignana Sakuntala.* You find more passages which are highly romantic as they seem to be erotic. Critics are not justified in saying that my works overdo scenes relating to love and sex.

PBR: Will you please comment on your theory of fiction?

RR: I have written puranas but not novels.

PBR: Have you ever taught your own creative writing to your students? If so, how did the students react to your works?

RR: I have taught only Indian philosophy. I never told

them about my writing.

PBR: To your knowledge, has any comprehensive bibliography appeared in the recent past? If so, can you give me the details?

RR: *The Journal of Commonwealth Literature, World Literature Today* seemed to have brought about some Bibliographies.

PBR: What advice do you give to young artists and critics from India?

RR: They have to practise writing as Sadhana.

Index